DATE DUE

DE 14 '99			
MR 20 '99			
AU 2/ '01			
DE 10 '01			
DE 13 '01			
MY 9 '02			
DE 17 '03			
JE 3 '06			

DEMCO 38-296

Counseling
to End
Violence
Against Women

To battered women, and especially to Nicole Brown.
May your lives contribute to a transformed world.

Counseling to End Violence Against Women

A Subversive Model

Mollie Whalen

SAGE Publications
International Educational and Professional Publisher
Thousand Oaks • London • New Delhi

Thousand Oaks, California 91320
E-mail: order@sagepub.com

SAGE Publications Ltd.
6 Bonhill Street
London EC2A 4PU
United Kingdom

SAGE Publications India Pvt. Ltd.
M-32 Market
Greater Kailash I
New Delhi 110 048 India

Printed in the United States of America

Library of Congress Cataloging-in-Publication Data

Whalen, Mollie.
  Counseling to end violence against women: a subversive model / by
    Mollie Whalen.
      p.cm.
  Includes bibliographical references and index.
  ISBN 0-8039-7379-9 (acid-free paper). — ISBN 0-8039-7380-2 (pbk.:
    acid-free paper)
  1. Abused women—Counseling of—United States.   2. Feminist
therapy—United States.   I. Title.
HV1445.W43   1996

362.82'9286'0973—dc20   95-50177

This book is printed on acid-free paper.

96 97 98 99   10 9 8 7 6 5 4 3 2 1

Cover Design: Candice Harman

Contents

Preface

When I began this book, the trial of O. J. Simpson was capturing the nation's attention. In the aftermath of that trial and the decision to acquit, we are wondering as much about the societal costs of racism as about the costs of woman battering. Guilty of murder or not, reasonable doubt or jury nullification, the acquittal of O. J. Simpson confirms every battered woman's worst fears: He's going to kill me. And he's going to get away with it. And there is nothing I can do.

Like many Americans, I was initially caught up in the spectacle surrounding the celebrity of the man charged with Nicole Brown's murder, her former husband, O. J. Simpson. As a sports fan and a Californian, I had "known" The Juice since the 1960s when he played for the University of Southern California. I followed his career as a professional with the Buffalo Bills and the San Francisco 49ers. After his retirement as a player, I continued to appreciate his commentaries as a sports announcer for a national network. And I, like the millions of Americans who watch television on a daily basis, admired this strong, good-looking, personable man as he ran through airports for Hertz. Of course, all I really knew about O. J. was the persona he projected through an image on television. Within a few days of the murder, the press began reporting the history of physical abuse that Nicole Brown had experienced over the course of her relationship with O. J. Simpson. Suddenly I "knew" Nicole Brown in a much deeper way than I had known O. J. Simpson. Prior to her murder, I was not even aware of her existence, yet I now knew Nicole Brown, because for many years I worked in daily contact with battered women. I know the fear, the pain, the sense of hopelessness and helplessness that battered women experience. I know this reality far more clearly than I could ever know a televised image.

My fascination with spectacle quickly turned to anger about society's failure to protect women. This focus has not only renewed my conviction that traditional psychology is inadequate in its response to battered women but has also raised questions for me again about some of the hallmarks of feminist psychology, in particular the notion of individual empowerment. I began to think about the ways in which Nicole Brown's life and death might be used as a catalyst to remold our conceptual tools for helping battered women. So I decided to write this book in which I offer a conceptual tool, a model for counseling battered women. I have shared the immediate context that prompted me to write this book; but as a feminist, I believe that any theory is developed by a person, a subject, within a social and historical context that has political implications. So let me begin by providing my personal context and history in more detail.

Much of my professional life has been devoted to working toward a society that respects and values women. For as long as I can remember, I have positioned myself as an advocate for social change. Long before I could begin to articulate just what I thought needed to change or how to go about it, I saw myself as opposed to a status quo that I equated with mediocrity. I knew that a much better world could be achieved. Perhaps this urge for change was merely adolescent idealism, restlessness, and oppositionality wrought by the circumstances of the 1960s. Certainly, my impulse to work for change emerged long before I encountered a feminist analysis that crystallized my unformulated ideas about political power and oppression. Nonetheless, I entered graduate school in 1978 with the explicit idea that the best way to work for social change was to work on changing individuals. It was my view that respecting, validating, and valuing individuals through the counseling relationship would cause these individuals to emerge with a changed consciousness about the world. Cumulatively, the changed consciousness of individuals would lead to the creation of a more just and equitable society. However, since 1978 I have gradually come to view this notion differently.

Many years and complex experiences intervened between the start of my master's degree program and the completion of my doctoral degree in counseling psychology. These experiences led me to identify myself as a radical feminist, a social activist, and a feminist psychologist, working toward fundamental changes in the way we structure our personal lives and our political and economic arrangements. These experiences also caused me to question my earlier assumption that focusing exclusively on individual changes in consciousness was enough to eventually change society. I began to think of myself as an activist connected to a social movement for women's liberation. These self-concepts have, over the past 20 years or so, become important elements of my identity as a woman and a professional.

From 1978 to 1990, I participated in the work of a community-based women's center in Pennsylvania that provides counseling and other services to battered women and sexual assault victims. I began as a hotline volunteer, responding to crisis calls, and later offered group and individual counseling to victims. When state and federal funding became available for domestic violence and sexual assault programs, I became a board member of this center and helped articulate its feminist philosophy and goals. In 1984, I was hired as executive director of the center. From this position I continued to work directly with victims but also trained and supervised the counseling and volunteer staff. I worked with the center's board of directors and staff to build on and find innovative ways to implement our philosophy while providing an increasingly utilized service for victims.

As the director of a rape and domestic violence program, part of my role was to serve as a board member for each of two state coalitions—the Pennsylvania Coalition Against Domestic Violence (PCADV) and the Pennsylvania Coalition Against Rape (PCAR). These coalitions serve as the funding conduits, information clearinghouses, monitors, and support systems for community rape and domestic violence programs across the state. In that role, I had the opportunity to be involved in many aspects of social policy planning and development. It was also at this level of participation that I first developed an affective sense of connection to a social movement—a sense of being part of something larger, joined with other women in a common effort to end violence against women.

Two experiences in particular stand out for me. These experiences solidified my sense of participation in a social movement and my commitment to the values and goals of that movement. As a board member of PCADV, I served on a committee whose task it was to develop a program model for battered women's programs. Once we had clarified that it was our mission to develop an ideal model to which programs might aspire, rather than a blueprint from which mandated standards would be developed, we were free to develop recommendations based in our strong ideological commitment, without regard to more conservative community, economic, or political constraints. On an ideological level, I felt closely aligned with the women on that committee who developed the program model, and I attempted to implement the model, as much as possible, in the program I directed.

A second experience of importance to me occurred in 1988. I attended the National Coalition Against Domestic Violence (NCADV) conference in Seattle. Many events at that conference stand out for me as building on my commitment to and participation in a battered women's movement, but one had particular relevance for me because it stimulated some questions that later became the basis for my dissertation thesis. I attended a feminist research group that met several times during the week of the conference. The goal of the group was to develop a research agenda for the battered women's movement. The idea was that rather than having our issues studied by academicians outside the movement, we would define and research those issues. In that way we could ensure that the research would be accountable to battered women. This notion was exciting but also created some dissonance for me because of the ways the group dichotomized academicians and participants in the movement. I saw myself as one who sought ways to combine my academic training with my activist commitments. At the time, I was able to set aside this dissonance and focus on study topics that were brainstormed within the group. One of the subjects identified included questions about what we (battered women's programs) were doing in counseling—what made it work and why was it good? These questions helped provide the spark for my dissertation research, in which I developed a descriptive model of the ways in which counselors working in rape and domestic violence programs conceptualized their counseling efforts, as well as the ideology of the social movement in which they worked (Whalen, 1992).

So, in the 15 years since I obtained my master's degree in clinical psychology, my encounters with radical feminist movements and with feminist political and psychological theory have deepened my commitment to social change. In recent years, I have moved from my position as an active participant in the battered women's movement to practice in a site of academic learning. I no longer direct a community-based women's center that works with battered women and survivors of sexual violence. Now I teach and theorize in women's studies and direct a university-based women's center, where my goal is to ensure that the feminist theories of women's studies remain connected to the practice of women's center services and programs. In this environment I still encounter, with a fair amount of regularity, women who are victims of male violence. And I work with them within the framework of the counseling model I will articulate in this book, remaining attentive to the ways my theories and ideology inform my counseling practice. I am better able to conceptualize and explicate the ways in which society permeates the individual and can be acted upon by the individual. I carry within me a powerful sense of community, developed through my participation in the anti-rape and battered women's movements specifically, and feminism more generally. And I continue to believe that social change is both imperative and possible. I remain convinced that one particularly powerful avenue for igniting the fire of social change ideals is the counseling relationship, particularly when the problems being explored through counseling are those that appear to be rooted in our social and political systems. This book is an outgrowth of these ideals and convictions.

There is, however, more that the reader should know about the context out of which my ideas developed about counseling as an activity aimed at subverting the status quo. In 1991, when I completed my dissertation research and described the conceptual models that emerged from the interviews I conducted, I discovered that the counseling models held by counselors working in battered women's and anti-rape programs were primarily psychological (i.e., focused on individual remediation) and apolitical. These models reminded me of the understandings I had held when I entered graduate school; however, because my views of counseling had changed radically through my experience in the battered women's movement, I had assumed the counselors who worked in movement programs also would have ideas about counseling as a political endeavor aimed at social change. I was surprised that there was a discrepancy between my findings and what I expected to discover, for they stood in stark contrast to the ideology of the battered women's movement.

As a participant in that movement, and a member of both PCADV and NCADV, I was initially reluctant to disseminate the findings of my dissertation research. My reluctance was based in part on what I encountered at the 1988 conference in Seattle—the tendency within NCADV to be wary of "professionalist" approaches to helping battered women. NCADV has historically attacked professionalism as antithetical to feminist responses to battered women. For NCADV, professionalism implies training in patriarchal institutions of academia, which cuts counselors off from a feminist consciousness about the societal roots of woman battering. Although I believed that I could merge my professional training and my activism, now that I was nearing the completion of my Ph.D., I could be defined as a professional. I feared my findings might be quickly dismissed, despite my years of work in the battered women's movement. Moreover, because my research revealed a disjunction between the ideology of the battered women's movement and the practice of counseling within domestic violence programs, I was also concerned that the counselors who were part of my study might be discredited.

My concerns about publishing my research went beyond my personal worry about being dismissed as a professional, and even beyond my consideration of the potential effects on my colleagues who participated in the study. I initially felt that my findings were, in a sense, a betrayal of NCADV and the battered women's movement. That is, I was concerned that the findings might be used as part of a conservative attack on the movement, and I wanted in no way to contribute to the backlash that feminist movements for social change are experiencing. But my response to the death of Nicole Brown has changed my attitudes. I have come to realize that the failure to disseminate my findings constitutes a far greater betrayal—a betrayal of battered women as a group.

And so it is within this context that I have taken the disappointment from my case study research, the horror and tragedy of Nicole Brown's abuse and murder, and my feminist commitments to radical social change and have developed a model for subversive counseling. Although I focus here on the concerns and needs of battered women, I believe the model can be extended to work with any persons whose presenting issues are the result of problems that are rooted in society. The model is grounded in the heritage of those theorists who offer a more holistic conceptualization of the practice of counseling and the practice of social change (Agel, 1971; Brown, 1994; Hutchinson & Sandler, 1975; Prilleltensky, 1994). It is within this tradition that I formulate and offer a radical feminist model for counseling to end violence against women.

Acknowledgments

This book is the product of many years of conceptual development, political experience, and psychological counseling practice. The specifics are detailed in the introduction to provide a basis for understanding the context out of which this subversive model of counseling arose. Here, I want to briefly provide formal acknowledgment of the people who have, knowingly or unknowingly, assisted me in this enterprise.

First, a word about the title of this book. I have long been convinced that counseling should promote social change, social justice, and a transformed world. Thus, *Counseling to End Violence Against Women* provides a counseling model that seeks to challenge and subvert, from a feminist perspective, the status quo. In arriving at an understanding that counseling could indeed serve subversive goals, I am indebted to the following people.

I acknowledge the social movement organized for and by battered women, and I am thankful for the experience I gained by participating in the work of the National Coalition Against Domestic Violence and the Pennsylvania Coalition Against Domestic Violence. A special acknowledgment is due the counselors who participated in my doctoral research project.

Berenice Fisher introduced me to alternative approaches to building psychological theory and encouraged me in my pursuit of women's studies, feminist criticism, and feminist activism. Mary Sue Richardson served as mentor and adviser during my doctoral study at New York University and supported my nontraditional (for psychology) research. Bernard Katz, professor, adviser, and longtime proponent of community action counseling, used the phrase *counseling as a subversive activity* in an earlier paper. Though I had arrived independently at the title for my dissertation, *Counseling as a Subversive Activity,* discovering that he and others had also seen the subversive potential of counseling provided a sense of validation for my work.

I have learned from the lives and struggles of three sisters who are my immediate forebears—my mother, Marion Geserich Townsend; my aunt, Jane Taylor; and my aunt, Ruth Reid—as well as their mother and my grandmother, Adelaide Geserich. My daughters, Erin and Kelly, also have taught me a great deal—about them and about myself. Each has experiences of resistance and tolerance, to patriarchal oppression as well as to their mother's strongly stated opinions.

My life partner, Joe Ashcroft, prodded me to write this book now. The time, he insisted, was right, and in the conversation about woman battering, my ideas were needed. I was convinced by his urging to begin. And now, thanks to his willingness to read and reread, to edit and re-edit, to continue to ask me what in the world I mean by *X,* it is done.

Counseling and Social Change

Jaime first came to the battered women's shelter when she was 28. The ER nurse had called the hotline worker when Jaime was to be discharged. Jaime had her three children with her. Her story was a familiar one. Jaime was married at 19 to an auto mechanic with big dreams; the beatings started when she became pregnant the first time. The cycle of abuse became well established over the next 9 years. The beatings would be followed by a phase of contrition and renewed romance. Then there would be a period in which Jaime was alternately ignored or denigrated for everything she did. Often her husband would disappear for several days at a time, offering no explanation when he returned, other than to charge Jaime with having driven him away. The three daughters Jaime gave birth to provided her some measure of comfort, but only seemed to exacerbate her husband's anger, moodiness, and abuse. This time he had tripped over a toy left in the hall. He flew into a rage about her messy housekeeping and started slapping her around. The neighbors called the police, but by the time they arrived, Jaime was badly bruised and her lips and eye were swollen.

When the staff counselor talked with her the following day, it was evident that Jaime not only had been beaten physically but also had been beaten down psychologically. She was listless and seemed uninterested in making decisions about her future. After a few days in shelter, she began thinking about going back home to more familiar surroundings. Her attitude was one of resignation. She expressed no particular hope for the relationship and no feelings of love or caring for her husband, though she did say she thought it was important for the children to have a father.

Jaime returned home; however, some kind of personal connection had been made with her counselor, and she expressed a desire to return for counseling on a weekly basis. The counselor continued to work with Jaime over the next year and a half, focusing on building her self-esteem and envisioning a better life—one free of abuse. Jaime responded to these interventions with increasing enthusiasm. She resurrected her childhood dream of becoming a nurse. She began to feel better about herself and much less tolerant of her husband's verbal abuse. She looked forward to the periods when he would ignore her or leave for several days.

Jaime met a man who was sympathetic to her situation. Touched by his attention, she began an affair and started thinking about leaving her husband. As Jaime began taking concrete steps to leave, her husband's attempts at control increased. She started a program designed to help homemakers define possible careers and develop plans for education and training. He refused to help with child care and he sabotaged her car. She took a part-time job in a doctor's office. Her husband stalked her and harassed her at work. She yelled back at him when he complained about her appearance and her laziness. He blackened her eye and broke her jaw.

That was the last time Jaime was to be beaten by this man. She gathered her children and came to shelter. She obtained a protection order. Within a few days, she had received emergency funds from welfare and a housing allotment from the Salvation Army. She found a place to rent, moved in, and began a new life.

The new life was not without difficulties. Her husband still occasionally harassed her. He was inconsistent with support payments. He refused to cooperate with a divorce. Finances were tight. Her lover decided he couldn't leave his wife, and Jaime ended the affair. But despite these difficulties and the responsibilities for raising three children, Jaime found the resources to enroll in an LPN program and move ahead with her life.

Today, Jaime seems very different from the battered woman who first came to shelter 3 years ago. Her affect is bright. Her confidence is increasing. She looks forward to working as a nurse and perhaps returning to school for an RN degree. She hopes to meet a man who will care for her and her children while allowing her the space to pursue her career and interests.

The counselor who worked with Jaime during this transformative period feels very happy for Jaime and all that she has accomplished. The counselor believes that her role was to be a companion and guide as Jaime discovered and rebuilt herself. Because the counselor provided information about the resources and options available to Jaime, when she finally felt ready to leave, she knew how to access material assistance to do so. The counselor empowered Jaime to develop into the person she could be by validating her experiences and demonstrating care and concern for her as a person.

Most of us who work in the helping professions of psychology, counseling, and social work would feel very satisfied with this outcome and would share the counselor's sense of pride in Jaime's accomplishments. Jaime has gotten free from an abusive relationship. She is much happier. She feels good about herself and sees a future for herself. But I ask myself, and I want you to ask yourself, what's missing from this picture?

I have worked with many individual battered women who have gotten free from their abusive relationships. Some wander into new relationships that seem only minor improvements to the ones they've left. Some, like Jaime, work more on developing themselves and do not seem as pressured to establish new relationships, though a happy marriage often remains an ultimate goal. I am happy to have helped any battered woman get free from an abusive relationship. But working as a counselor in this piecemeal fashion—helping one individual woman after another get free—leaves me with a sense of impotence regarding the massive social problem of woman battering.

A woman is battered in the United States every 18 seconds (U.S. Department of Justice, 1986). If all the counselors in America were working to help battered women, we would not be able to stem the tide of this problem. As soon as we help one woman get free, another is there to take her place as the abuser's punching bag. No, as those of us who define ourselves as feminists agree, woman battering is a social problem that requires social solutions.

For many years, I worked as a counselor within a battered women's movement that recognizes the social dimensions of woman battering. The goal of this movement is to end male violence against women. To accomplish that goal, the movement agitates for social and political change. It seeks to radicalize battered women to help themselves and others by speaking out about their abuse; lobbying political institutions for just, protective laws and practices; and complaining about the treatment of women whenever we are confronted with barriers and inequities. At least this is the theory and the spirit of the battered women's movement. But as activists, we have not always been able to make the transition from our social analysis and our ideological fervor to the everyday work of sitting and talking to an individual battered woman.

What is missing from the counseling Jaime experienced? It is not that a feminist analysis of battering was absent, for Jaime probably did hear that she was not alone in this problem. She probably did talk with the counselor about how she was socialized as a girl, how this affected her life goals and expectations, and how similar this experience was to other women's experience. What was likely missing from the counseling was the active connection between this analysis, the need for radical social change, and the use of counseling as an opportunity to join with other women in seizing and practicing power. Jaime was empowered to develop a different sense of herself and to make personal changes in her life situation, rather than encouraged to take power by acting against the root sources of her problem, of women's problem—male violence against women.

These are the issues I explore throughout the remainder of this book: the need for our social change analysis to be connected to our counseling practice; the reasons for the disjuncture between theories of change, theories of counseling, and the practice of counseling; and the possibilities for changing our counseling practice so that it serves the goals of a radical feminist vision for social change. I plan to lay a framework for a counseling model for working with battered women that is unapologetically political and subversive in its focus and intent. I will argue that the practice of counseling ought to be informed by and guided by one's ideology about an ideal society and the means to achieve that vision. Therefore, we need a counseling model that keeps the definition of the social problem, the vision of an ideal world, the means of achieving that vision, and the guiding philosophy of that vision coherently aligned with one another—a model that reflects and operationalizes this ideology in the counseling work with clients. I will argue that we cannot resort to the kind of traditional psychology that reflects an individualism and humanism that makes battered women ultimately responsible for their battering and for changing their situation. Instead, we must acknowledge that all women are responsible for battered women and for social change to eliminate violence against women, because woman battering affects us all as women. We need a counseling model that focuses not on the empowerment of individual women but on seizing power collectively as women; that is, we need a political model of counseling. We need a model that focuses on subverting the existing social system, rather than a model that focuses on helping individual women change their individual situations. We need a model in which our primary counseling goal is eliminating violence against women in the world.

These ideas for connecting counseling to social change are not emerging here for the first time. In the early 1990s, I began to search the literature for theories related to the kind of radical and feminist social change counseling that I was expecting to find in my proposed research with counselors in battered women's programs. It was not easy to find what I was looking for. I first examined the literature in counseling psychology, the area in which I was pursuing doctoral study. After all, I was initially attracted to counseling psychology over clinical psychology because of its philosophy of conceiving clients as basically healthy, rather than suffering from pathological mental illnesses, and because of its support for understanding the social context of psychological problems. I read a great deal, searching for what I thought others must have considered before I came to the field. I read some incisive critiques of traditional psychology, perhaps the most important among those were several articles by Edward Sampson (1977, 1978, 1981). But I found nothing suggesting that psychologists ought to find ways of engaging their clients in political analysis and action.

I turned to the field of community psychology, which I knew had evolved out of opposition to hospital-based psychological treatment approaches. I was aware that the emphasis of community psychology was on prevention in the community—treating the community systems that often created psychological symptoms. But in reviewing this literature, I decided that community psychology had never realized its radical potential (Scribner, 1968). Although community psychology did try to emphasize

prevention, it basically relied on a medical model approach to understanding psychological problems and treatment.

I next sought out the social work literature, for social work is a field
that is theoretically devoted to understanding and changing the social
systems in which individuals must function. I found some interesting
pieces from the 1970s that argued for radical social work. Some equated
radical with *Marxist* and contended that a Marxist revolution was necessary (Galper, 1980). Others criticized some of the radical impulses of
social work as simplistic (Bailey & Brake, 1975), but held that counseling
should include action for change in the systemic roots of individual
problems (Galper, 1980; Rose, 1972). Martin Rein's (1970) analysis of
theories of social change and the need to connect intervention strategies
with the purposes of the intervention was helpful in that he ultimately
promotes a radical social policy approach to social work. This approach
is based in a radical creed, a commitment to reducing inequalities by
altering the political, economic, and social conditions as a precondition
to individual change; however, he continues to separate action for social
policy changes from casework activities with clients.

For me, a crucial problem with these earlier radical social work approaches was that they failed to include a gendered analysis of social
problems. The combination of separating social policy action from casework activities and failing to provide a gendered analysis seriously weakened
the radical potential of these theories. In addition, though I found many
of the insights useful, I realized the extent to which social work has failed
to influence my discipline. Graduate programs in clinical and counseling
psychology seldom include social work literature on their reading lists.
This is unfortunate, especially because social work programs do include
psychology literature on their reading lists. The absence of references to
radical social work in counseling psychology also contributed to my
difficulty in locating theoretical roots for my counseling model.

In reviewing the domains of literature that pertained to the activity of
counseling, I occasionally came across a reference to Seymour Halleck.
He was cited as criticizing traditional psychotherapy, which he suggested
served to strengthen the status quo rather than challenge a problematic
social system. This seemed to be closer to what I was looking for. I tracked
down Halleck's *The Politics of Therapy* (1971) and discovered a group of
critics known as the antipsychiatrists (cf. Cooper, 1967; Laing, 1967;
Steiner, 1975; Szasz, 1970). The antipsychiatrists were psychiatrists who

in various ways began challenging traditional notions of mental illness and advancing new ideas about the social genesis of personal problems. This body of work was somewhat interesting, but again had the fatal flaw of ignoring gender and women's oppression. In any case, psychiatry plays a somewhat different role than psychology does in our culture, and I was looking for what my own profession, psychology, had to say on this important topic. Finally, in reading the antipsychiatrists, I found references to Jerome Agel, who had edited a book in 1971 called *The Radical Therapist*. It was not a simple task to find a copy of Agel's book, but it turned out that this was definitely what I had been looking for.

Radical therapy emerged from the burgeoning critique of the institution of psychotherapy that began in the 1960s. In the late 1960s, two independent groups emerged, both calling themselves radical therapists. One group started with a radical psychiatry course offered by Claude Steiner and Hogie Wyckoff, a feminist activist, through the Free University in Berkeley, California. This conjoining of antipsychiatry, radical therapy, and feminism is perhaps the first evidence of the historical connection between these theoretical schools. Steiner and Wyckoff formed a radical therapy collective that focused on eliminating the hierarchy of the therapeutic relationship between client and counselor. The collective combined this philosophical emphasis with the techniques of transactional analysis (Steiner, 1975). Included in the collective were activists from the Insane Liberation Front, a group of former psychiatric patients who considered themselves victims of mental health treatments such as electroshock, drug therapies, and involuntary confinement (Sipe, 1982). A second group, in North Dakota, also formed a radical therapist collective but eventually decided that being a radical and being a therapist were mutually exclusive (Hutchinson & Sandler, 1975). With this change in political awareness, the collective shifted from a focus on the therapeutic relationship to a focus on actively aiding liberation groups and all oppressed people.

The assumptions and theory behind radical therapy were summarized by Agel (1971) in *The Radical Therapist*. He contended that alienation is the root of all psychological problems, and that it results from oppression. Radical therapy starts from an "awareness that therapy is a social and political event, and moves to the conviction that therapy systems—like many of this country's institutions—must be changed" (Agel, p. ix). Much of the theoretical basis of feminist counseling theory can be found in the radical therapy literature. Feminist counseling approaches, when they first emerged in the 1970s, used an analysis similar to radical therapy's analysis of oppression as the root of alienation, applying it specifically to the condition of women: Women were oppressed and therefore alienated from patriarchal society. It was this alienation that led to psychological problems. Though the radical therapy literature has occasionally been referred to as a source of feminist theorizing in psychology (cf. Holroyd, 1976; Richardson & Johnson, 1984), there is typically no thorough exploration of this connection.[1] Yet radical therapy established a social and political emphasis that was quickly adopted by early feminist therapists. Radical therapy provided an analysis of the power relationship between client and therapist, a social structural analysis of oppression, and an emphasis on group work—all important elements of feminist therapy. Another area emphasized by radical therapy was the incorporation of social activism in therapy, that is, encouraging the client to engage in social change activities.

Though feminist therapy typically acknowledges the importance of social change for women as a group, much of the current theory de-emphasizes that element in the actual clinical interactions with clients. One reason for the drift away from a strong emphasis on including social change activities in counseling was the growing influence of humanistic psychology and a gradual disconnection of feminist therapy from its historical roots in radical therapy. Feminist therapists have increasingly turned to humanistic ideas about personal empowerment and individual growth. There are also fundamental conflicts in feminist therapies that try to merge a social change analysis with a humanist model of individual growth and development.

Still, some grassroots feminist groups have developed models for helping that purportedly include political activism as part of counseling. The battered women's movement is one example of a radical feminist group that advocates for counseling as a tool for social activism; however, my research in the early 1990s exposed me to the reality that even in these radical feminist programs, counselors are not, in practice, using counseling to subvert the social systems that sustain violence against women. So even when our models theoretically support the kind of political action and political seizing of power that I maintain we must consider, those models need to be better understood and implemented by counselors.

As a result of these experiences and considerations, I determined to develop a subversive counseling model. By *subversive counseling* I mean counseling in which a radical feminist theory and vision of social change is connected to the process and activity of helping. The goals of this subversive counseling model are to identify the social roots of women's problems, to connect women clients with other women working to eradicate or transform those roots, and to work toward a society in which women and men can participate as equal partners in all spheres. Feminist subversive counseling is to be contrasted with two other approaches to counseling. Traditional paternalistic counseling (whether based in the theories of psychoanalysis, behaviorism, or humanism) helps women clients adjust to problematic situations that oppress and violate them as individuals. This approach serves to reinforce and reproduce the oppression of all women. The second approach, feminist humanist counseling, functions to empower individual women to change their self-perceptions and gain the strength to change their problematic situations. Neither of these approaches directly challenges or tries to alter the social origins of women's problems.

My history of work with battered women led me to focus this subversive counseling model on battered women. My goal is that counselors who use the model will be able to connect individual battered women to the feminist movement to end male violence against all women. Moreover, the model will encourage battered women to work on the social roots of their problem. I am not asserting that the model I will propose is the only possible one for successfully working with battered women. Whenever we engage in counseling with individuals, the individual context and needs must be taken into account. But I do maintain that such a model needs to be part of the repertoire of any feminist who claims to be working with or on behalf of battered women. I assert this because I also believe that a counseling model that is focused on social change ultimately results in individual battered women who are healed, who feel good about themselves, who are better able to implement effective decisions, and who do not need to rely on abusive men.

The model will require refinement and additions, but I firmly believe in its essential components and maintain that it needs to be among those models considered for conceptualizing the work with battered women. This subversive counseling model will help address the inconsistency between ideology and practice in the battered women's movement, will encourage feminist therapists to reappropriate their radical history and question the implicit conserving nature of humanism, and will challenge professional schools of psychology and counseling to broaden their traditional individualistic focus of training, particularly when it comes to human problems that are rooted in society.

The rest of this book is organized to take the reader through the necessary groundwork to thoroughly understand the need and the rationale for and the issues involved in developing and implementing such a model. Let me be clear about this point. I believe that one of the fundamental problems facing feminism in general and the battered women's movement in particular is a disconnection between our theory and our practice. This is especially true for those of us involved in counseling. Our vision for a world without sexism is often not connected to our theories of counseling and social change, which in turn are not connected to our counseling practices. I have arranged this book to make those connections explicit. Though this book is about counseling practices with battered women, it is not a practice manual. Therefore, I do not present the model and then offer case studies and application techniques for various situations. I am offering instead a theoretical model, built from and grounded in feminist movements for social change and the practice of counselors in battered women's programs. For you to grasp the context and theoretical considerations from which this model was developed, I must first provide that background and discuss the debated issues that affect the development of a politically subversive approach to counseling. The model itself is not presented until Chapter 7. Though you might be thoroughly familiar with pieces of the grounding I provide in the earlier chapters, I believe that if you were to read Chapter 7 now, it would neither convince you of the need to consider this model nor allow you to grasp the essentials of the way in which it was developed. More important, you would be isolating the practice from the theory. Thus, you would not be able to implement the model in a meaningful and transformative fashion.

In the following chapter, I review a classification system for differing feminist analyses and their resulting political projects. In Chapter 3, I discuss some of the debated issues in feminism that can differentially affect our approaches to counseling and consider them in relation to the emergence of feminist therapy. I also raise questions about some of the central tenets in feminist therapy and underscore the conflicts between humanist and radical feminist approaches. In Chapter 4, I consider the radical potential of the battered women's movement and the ways in which that potential is sometimes subverted. Chapter 5 provides a review of the feminist theories for understanding and counseling battered women, and Chapter 6 summarizes my case study of counselors who work with battered women every day. Chapter 7 then outlines a social vision, an ideological model for social change, and a subversive counseling model that connects theory to practice. In the final chapter, I urge the battered women's movement, graduate schools of counseling, and you, the reader, to "carry it on" by actively using this model whenever you believe the roots of a client's problems lie in society.

Note

1. Bonnie Burstow (1992) does acknowledge the contributions of the antipsychiatrists as one strand of influence on radical feminist therapy; however, she identifies radical therapy, another strand of influence, as arising out of the practice and theory of transactional analysis. I think this way of framing the development of radical therapy is misconstrued. It is true that Claude Steiner, an antipsychiatrist, and Hogie Wyckoff, a feminist, practiced therapy together within the theoretical framework of transactional analysis (Wyckoff, 1975). And they did come to define their work as radical therapy. But to give credit to transactional analysis for the emergence of radical therapy seems to me an error, because the theory of transactional analysis is little more than psychoanalysis in lay language. In and of itself, transactional analysis offers no insight into the social construction of psychological and social problems.

Movements for
Women's Liberation

The history of women's social change movements is centuries old.
Much of that history is an exciting story for people who remain
committed to working toward a society in which women will share power
equally with men and be able to live in a world free of violence. A brief
summary of the history and ideologies of the U.S. women's movement
over the past 30 years will establish the context for the emergence of the
battered women's movement in this country and is important to the project
of grounding a subversive counseling model.

The beginnings of this period, often referred to as *second wave feminism*
(Lear, 1968), occurred from the late 1960s to the late 1970s. This was a
decade of widespread social ferment in the United States, as the student
new left protested the Vietnam war, black militants promoted black pride
and power, gay and lesbian groups rallied around the Stonewall incident,
and the women's liberation movement emerged.

The history of women's movements in the United States, before the
emergence of the second wave, is by and large a history of women striving

for access to the rights, status, and power available to men as a group. These social actions grew out of a philosophy of liberalism, based in the notion that women, like men, are rational human beings who have the right and responsibility to act as citizens, with maximum freedom from governmental interference and maximum protection of individual rights. A clear example of this phenomenon is the women's suffrage movement that successfully obtained the vote for women with the passage of the 19th Amendment.

These successes, combined with the development of an economic depression followed by a world war, produced a quieting of feminist activism for a few decades. But by 1960, women were beginning to agitate again for reforms that would permit equal opportunity and participation in our democratic-capitalist system. It was the emergence of this second wave women's liberation movement that spawned other women-focused social action groups, such as the battered women's movement.

Many books have been written describing the history of second wave feminism in the United States (cf. Deckard, 1979; Freeman, 1995) and the distinctive ideologies of various feminist perspectives (cf. Echols, 1989; Jaggar, 1983).[1] Knowledge of the broader parameters of these sometimes fine ideological distinctions is important for understanding the radical and subversive potential of both the battered women's movement and feminist counseling practice.

The profusion of feminist political organizing in the 1960s and 1970s paralleled the profusion of emerging philosophical distinctions and emphases among different groups of feminists, resulting in labels that were used to help distinguish among the various groups. Liberal feminists, Marxist or politico feminists, radical feminists, socialist feminists, cultural feminists, women's liberationists, and just plain feminists were all labels applied to different groups. Superimposed on these categories, lesbian and black feminists also claimed their own distinctive ideologies. These philosophical and group distinctions have been categorized in various ways. The taxonomy used here—liberal feminism, radical feminism, socialist feminism, and cultural feminism—is simplified to permit broad comparisons among schools of feminist thought that imply markedly different political strategies and aims.

Liberal Feminism

Liberal feminism emerged from liberal philosophy and its concomitants, capitalism and democracy, and formed the basis of feminist political action before the development of radical feminist groups. From a liberalism perspective, human nature is defined by its rationality. Rational individual humans come together to form society. Liberal political theory is based in the concept of egalitarianism; that is, everyone is entitled to a fair share (of rights and opportunity), with maximum freedom from interference by other individuals and government. Because they do not differ in this essential human capacity to reason, men and women ought to participate as equals in society. The fact of male dominance in society is explained by irrational prejudice and can be overcome by rational arguments about women's equality to men. Women's oppression is defined as unjust discrimination against women. Liberal feminists accept the basic premises and values of our liberal, democratic society and support the existing governmental and institutional structures, except as they exclude women from equal rights and opportunities in the public sphere. The political project of liberal feminists is primarily to reform the existing societal structures to provide women equal rights and opportunities to participate in public life. Political activities of liberal feminists might include running for political office, lobbying legislators for changes in certain laws or policies that affect women, or advocating for salary equity for women in the workforce.

Radical Feminism

Radical feminists argue that the first historical and most significant oppression is the sex-class system. That is, long before social classes emerged within human societies, there was a division of labor, power, and value according to the classification of humans by sex. These divisions established a sex-class system that granted men power over women, prescribed specific social roles to men and to women, and differentially valued those roles to the relative detriment of women. Although there may have existed some societies—in remote historical times or geographical locations—that did not operate under these patriarchal values and structures, by and large the major civilizations of Europe, Africa, and Asia, as well as those derivatives transported to and adopted by societies in North and South America and other parts of the world, can be described as patriarchal (i.e., relying on the rule of the father, or male).

Radical feminists seek to eradicate the root causes of women's oppression by arguing that men and women are, or have the potential to be, essentially the same—biologically, psychologically, socially, and politically. Thus, radical feminists work for the elimination of the patriarchy and all patriarchal forms of oppression. Radical feminists do not accept at face value the idea that our liberal, capitalist, democratic society is necessarily one that will work best for women, given a few modifications. For just as liberal philosophy originally left women out by defining them as irrational and thereby acted to support women's oppression, so too has democracy in practice often left women out, by excluding them from voting, holding office, and participating in public life. Similarly, capitalism has specific oppressive practices, aimed at women, that support women's oppression and men's privilege. The political project of radical feminists, therefore, is to work actively at subverting the existing political system and developing radically new societal forms.

Socialist Feminism

Socialist feminism is a synthesis, in many ways, of radical feminism and traditional Marxism. Socialist feminism views capitalism, male dominance, racism, and imperialism as intertwined, so that "the abolition of any of these systems requires the end of them all" (Jaggar, 1983, p. 124). Socialist feminism uses the method of historical materialism to analyze the ways in which human nature is created through the dialectic interaction of biology and social environment in particular social and historical contexts. These feminists extend the traditional Marxist definitions of praxis, labor, and production to include the "private" sphere— reproduction and consumption. They understand differences of age, sex, class, and race by examining the sexual division of labor within such groups.

Many radical feminists have argued that there is not a crucial difference between the socialist feminist position and the radical feminist position, because both assert the need for radical social change to eradicate systems of oppression and benefit women. However, socialist feminism has provided an effective counter to the charge leveled against radical feminism that it was developed by and for white middle-class women and that their analysis left other women, particularly women of color, on the margins. Socialist feminism, whether perceived as distinct from, subsumed by, or subsuming radical feminism, has certainly aided the cause of women's liberation by focusing attention on multiple systems of oppression and dominance and their interactive effect on women in varying circumstances and historical periods. The political project of socialist feminists is to subvert not only the patriarchal structures of oppression but also its racist, classist, heterosexist, ageist, and ableist structures.

Cultural Feminism

Cultural feminism is a much debated term. It was perhaps coined by Brooke Williams (1978), a radical feminist who was critical of the changing nature of radical feminism. Ellen Willis (1984) has also used the term, in a critical manner similar to its use by Williams. Although many women have used terms such as *women's culture* (Morgan, 1975), *female culture* (Burris, 1973), and *cultural revolution* (Radicalesbians, 1971), it appears that *cultural feminism* is not a term generated by the group of feminists to whom it is often applied. It is important to acknowledge the problem in using a term that the referenced group does not embrace, particularly if one supports the principle of self-determination for social groups. There are, however, critical differences between radical feminists and this other group, sufficient to warrant a distinction being made. For Alice Echols (1989), the primary distinction between radical and cultural feminism is that radical feminism was "a political movement dedicated to eliminating the sex-class system, but cultural feminism was a countercultural movement aimed at reversing the cultural valuation of the male and the devaluation of the female" (p. 6).

This grouping of feminist ideology evolved out of several debated issues within radical feminism and became fairly well defined as a category by the mid-1970s. The distinctive ideology of cultural feminism includes the following. First, cultural feminism reifies male-female differences by embracing either biological essentialism or a psychological determinism that values women's "natural" qualities (e.g., nurturance, emotionality, peacefulness, interdependence) over those of men (e.g., aggressiveness, rationality, independence, and arrogance). In addition, many cultural feminists promote a kind of separatism or counterculture for the development of women's communities and women's culture. In doing so, they view the counterculture experience as sufficient political action—if they indeed define it as political action at all. Moreover, cultural feminism emphasizes individual consciousness change over systemic political action. Finally, there is often within cultural feminism a promotion of women's spirituality. There seems to be a connection between these lines of thought and the recent burgeoning of New Age philosophies and culture, all of which are notable for their emphasis on individual responsibility for one's material situation and experiences and tend to lead to an apolitical stance with regard to social change. Cultural feminism, then, is the apolitical, spiritual, self-absorbed segment of feminists who have given up on political action and radical social change and have established safe havens of women's communities to promote woman-defined identities and "cultures."

Feminists from each of these ideological perspectives have made significant contributions to the theories and practices of the women's liberation movement as a whole and its offshoots, including the battered women's movement.

The Battered Women's Movement

Woman battering is a global phenomenon that occurs in many cultures and affects most of the world's population of women. Over the past 30 years, woman battering has become increasingly recognized as a problem, and women in many countries have organized to advocate for change. My personal involvement, however, has been in the movement in the United States and particularly in the programs found in Pennsylvania. So it is in analyzing the movement in this country that I can most effectively blend a discussion of theory with a discussion of practice.

The phenomenon of women being battered in intimate relationships has been referred to as "the problem that had no name." Indeed, one of the more important contributions of second wave feminism was the labels it provided to previously unnamed, largely unspoken, taboo problems that women confronted. Without a label to refer to a phenomenon, that phenomenon is extremely difficult to describe, to discuss, to count, and to analyze. When Erin Pizzey in Great Britain began talking about battered women (Pizzey, 1974), when Betsy Warrior in Boston began talking about wifebeating (Warrior, 1976), and when Del Martin in California first wrote about domestic violence (Martin, 1976), women at last had a name for something that women had experienced for thousands of years, something that was taken for granted because it had not been separated out from experience and named.

Since the 1970s, the term *domestic violence* has become the most popular and widely used phrase to refer to the phenomenon. Indeed, the national organization that embodies the battered women's movement in the United States is incorporated as the National Coalition Against Domestic Violence (though it also refers to itself as the Battered Women's Movement). And many of the state coalitions assume "domestic violence" in their titles. However, from a radical feminist perspective, there is a problem with using such a gender-neutral term to refer to a phenomenon that is primarily abuse and battering directed at women by men. The term *domestic violence,* though it purports to denote abuse in the home, obscures both the social and the gendered dimensions of the problem. And as Ann Jones points out, "it makes the violence sound domesticated" (quoted in Jacobs, 1994). Warrior's (1976) term, *wifebeating,* was a conscious attempt to more specifically name the problem as a women's problem, a social problem enabled by the institution of marriage. Later analyses pointed out, however, that women don't have to be wives in order to be beaten in intimate relationships. Often women live with men in relationships that are not legally recognized as marriage. Moreover, as more recent studies have shown, women can be beaten in relationships in which the couple is not cohabiting (dating relationships) or even in relationships with other women. And increasingly in battered women's programs, the definition of domestic violence has been extended to include what some have referred to as emotional or psychological abuse, sometimes without accompanying physical abuse. The phenomenon, in each of these situations, is at one level defined by the same dynamics—that is, violence and abuse directed at women, which serves to control women through the exertion of patriarchal power. In short, by this analysis, woman battering (including emotional abuse) in intimate relationships can be seen as a subset of the larger societal problem of violence against women (by men). Violence against women may be seen as a continuum of experiences, including sexual assault, incest, pornography, sexual harassment, and the ogling, comments, and catcalls that women are subjected to every day.

Violence against women, overall, is a threat experienced by every woman and so serves as a mechanism of controlling all women's behavior. By this analysis, all women are harmed by the fact that many women are violated; all men benefit from the fact that some men do violence against women.

Although I tend to consider domestic violence a euphemism for *woman battering in intimate relationships,* I sometimes use the term when referring to popular understandings of the phenomenon, to professional concepts that specifically employ the term, or to the national and state coalitions against domestic violence. However, when discussing the feminist social movement organized to address this problem, I will always refer to the *battered women's movement.* NCADV foregrounds the movement as one composed of battered women who are taking power for themselves, suggesting solutions out of their experiences, and offering help to other battered women.

The historical facts about the development of these women's movements and the organizational growth of the battered women's programs (see Appendix) are not generally disputed. Even the broad classification system of feminist perspectives offered here is widely accepted, though some would offer additional categories or draw the boundaries of ideological thought somewhat differently. Within feminism generally, however, as well as within the battered women's movement, conflicts and ideological debates are frequent. The details of such debate can be painstakingly precise, often appearing to be more an exercise in splitting hairs than an effort to offer workable solutions to social ills. But because I am convinced that effective practical solutions to problems must be grounded in carefully considered theory, an exploration of several of these issues, as they relate to feminist counseling and politics, is in order.

Note

1. See the Appendix for an overview of the historical events that marked the growth of U.S. second wave feminism and the battered women's movement, both nationally and in Pennsylvania.

Debated Issues in Feminism and the Emergence of Feminist Therapy

The variety of feminist perspectives that emerged throughout the first decade of second wave feminism led to differing recommendations for social change. Liberal feminists favored working within the existing social and political system for reforms to benefit women. Radical and social feminists argued for eradicating the existing system and developing new nonoppressive forms. Cultural feminists favored the creation of separate woman-defined systems. Within feminism, therefore, there were many debated issues affecting the development of approaches to therapy and counseling that came to be defined by feminist practitioners as feminist therapy. Ultimately, these debated issues also have significant import for the development of a subversive counseling model for battered women.

Male-Female Differences

One of the first questions that must be answered in any feminist analysis is how we understand and account for the observed differences between women and men. Those differences include social and material differences, such as differential participation in the public and private spheres or differential access to power (education, careers, wealth, politics); psychological differences, such as the inclination to nurture others or the ability to view oneself as separate and independent from others; and biological differences, such as differences in reproductive capacity or in physical size and strength. Varying understandings of each class of differences—social-material, psychological, and biological—create varying arguments both about what can be changed and what might need to be changed in order to make the world a safer and more equitable place for women. The arguments are not mutually exclusive; they build on one another.

Most people could probably agree that in much of U.S. history there have been clear differences between women and men in the social roles they enact. Women typically have had more responsibility and work within the private sphere—taking care of the house, attending to the children, preparing the meals. Men, until recently, have had more responsibility and work within the public sphere, viewing themselves as the primary family breadwinners and serving in leadership roles within businesses, institutions, and government. Some of these differences have been attenuated by distinctions of race, class, or sexual orientation. For example, poor black women have often had to work outside the home for the family to survive economically; single women and lesbians have often needed to be self-supporting.

Perhaps not quite as many people, but probably the majority, would agree that the social status and material benefits that accrue to those gender-defined roles have been different as well. Men's roles have been positively valued—better paid and more highly esteemed—over women's roles, whether women's roles are enacted primarily in the private sphere or in the workplace.

How do people account for these differences? Some would account for the differences described above in terms of biology. From this perspective, women are naturally (biologically) suited to staying at home, raising children, cooking meals, and cleaning houses. And men are naturally (biologically) suited to leaving the home, going out into the world, and bringing home the bacon. After all, the argument goes, men are typically stronger and swifter than women. They can labor more intensively for short periods than women can. For those who account for the differences in terms of psychology, women are socialized to care for others and they have developed intrapsychic structures that encourage loving empathy, interdependence, and nurturing. Therefore, women want to enact the roles they do at home. Moreover, women do not like to compete, a psychological trait that inhibits effective performance in the workplace. Men, on the other hand, are aggressive and like to compete, so they enjoy the give-and-take of the public sphere. Still others would account for the observed differences between the sexes in terms of power differentials between men and women, and women's historical oppression by men. From this perspective, women are kept at home or in underpaid or part-time jobs because this serves men's interests. Furthermore, society has created socialization practices and the resultant psychological internalization of gender that also serve men's interests. Violence against women is a mechanism of control to keep women in their proper place.

Political conservatives who oppose the feminist project in any of its forms tend to rely on biological explanations of the differences between men and women. From this perspective, not only do men and women differ in their reproductive capacities (the essential difference), but they differ in size, strength, and activity levels, in ability to reason logically, in emotionality, in intelligence, and so on and on. The social roles that women have in our society are the ones they are biologically suited to—mothering, cleaning, cooking, perhaps nursing and teaching. To counter this argument, Shulamith Firestone (1970), an early radical feminist theorist, suggested that the only important biological difference between women and men is women's capacity to bear and nurse children. Furthermore, she argued that technology had freed (or would soon free) women from the biological role and obligation to reproduce in order to continue the species. Not only did she foresee the possibility of test-tube babies (à la Huxley's *Brave New World*), but she pointed to the increasing ability of women to control their reproductive choices through contraceptives and abortion.

Feminists in psychology and biology have also spent a great deal of time countering the conservative argument for women's biological roles. They have undertaken new research and reanalyzed and challenged the existing body of sex differences research. As a result of this examination, many feminists would argue that although there are minor biological differences between men and women, our culture has built a massive edifice of social differentiation and discrimination on those very minor differences. More recently, other feminists, aware of the 20th-century emphases on the social construction of truth (cf. Unger, 1988, 1990), have challenged the very bases of the biological differences argument, asserting that all knowledge—including our knowledge about biology—is socially constructed and that we, in effect, make up this biological distinction by sex in the first place. They suggest that sex (the systematic division of people into one of two categories, male or female) is an artificial social construct and that the biological reality is a continuum of genetic and morphological possibilities. The feminist project then becomes the eradication of the two-gender system, the achievement of psychological androgyny, and the elimination of sex roles. Moreover, we ought to strive for acceptance and appreciation of this diversity in biological sexuality.

Cultural feminists, however, have tended to embrace the biological and psychological understandings of the differences between men and women. From their perspective, the social problem women encounter is not the differences per se but rather the differential value placed on those differences. In our culture, men's capacities are valued while women's are devalued. The goal of cultural feminists is the revaluing of women's capacities and women's nature and the effort to reverse (or for some, to equalize) the current differential valuing of men and women. Examples of this project might include the work of Mary Daly (1973, 1978) and Susan Griffin (1980), who define women's biology or essential nature as the solution to oppression and other ills of the world. Others assert women's special ways of knowing (Belenky, Clinchy, Goldberger, & Tarule, 1986), women's differential moral reasoning based in an ethic of care (Gilligan, 1982), and women's peaceful nature, developed out of the experience of mothering (Ruddick, 1980, 1983). These characteristics are offered as a model for developing a transformed world.

Liberal feminists have tended to argue that although there may be some biological and psychological differences between women and men, those differences are unimportant because women and men are equal in the essential human capacity to reason. Therefore, when women choose to enter the public sphere, they should be afforded an equal playing ground with men. Men should be able to choose to stay at home and care for the house, raise children, and cook. Liberal feminists, by focusing on the right of individuals to choose roles and lifestyles, reinforce the public-private split in our lives and ignore the idea that such "choices" are material circumstances forced from limited options and narrowed perspectives. Moreover, if men do not "choose" to stay at home or help at home, women have little basis for insisting that men share in the work of consumption and reproduction.

Radical feminists and social feminists argue that it is important to consider the power discrepancies between classes and the ways in which power is used to privilege some groups and oppress others. Initially, socialist feminists favored a focus on social classes in their analysis, feminist women of color favored a focus on race classes, and radical feminists favored a focus on sex classes. Eventually, however, there developed a more inclusive analysis that considered the interacting effects of various class divisions within society—not only sex classes but also social class, race, and sexual orientation. As those analyses became increasingly complex, politically radical feminists began to consider additional groups of less privileged women in our society, for example, older women, children, women with disabilities, and fat women. Currently, within radical feminism, we are dealing with the politics of multiple identities and the problems of remaining connected across our divisions, although analyses about gender remain primary within each of these divisions.

Differences Among Women

In focusing on the differences between men and women, feminism has been criticized for ignoring the differences among women. One of the central conceptual categories for feminists is that of *woman*. In the effort to conceptualize women as a class, early radical feminists stressed the commonalities among women's experiences. But critics argue that to a large extent those commonalities were falsely universalized from white middle-class experience to other cultures and experiences. Early radical feminists were taken to task for equating their notions of woman with that of white, middle-class heterosexual women. One of the dangers in losing sight of this diversity is that counseling can become a practice and a service exclusively for white, middle-class heterosexual women.

In 1977, the Combahee River Collective published a statement of black feminism, arguing that all the major systems of oppression—racism, sexism, classism, and heterosexism—are interlocking and must be targeted for political action. That statement remains today the clearest statement of purpose for politically active radical and socialist feminists. Similarly, bell hooks (1981) has urged women of color to reappropriate (white) feminism in order to create a "feminist ideology uncorrupted by racism" (p. 151). Gloria Anzaldua (Moraga & Anzaldua, 1983), Cherrie Moraga (1981), Audre Lorde (1984), Angela Davis (1981), and Barbara Smith (1985), among others, have also contributed to this discussion of racism in the movement. As a whole, radical feminism today has responded positively to these criticisms and continues to work toward understanding and including the variety of women's experiences and to making its services, including battered women's programs and counseling, responsive to the needs of diverse women.

In a somewhat analogous manner, lesbian feminists, who have been involved in the women's movement from its inception, have criticized the movement for its heterosexism and homophobia. Lesbian feminists have often not felt free to identify themselves within the movement and within certain movement organizations. Suzanne Pharr (1988) points out that lesbians have been subject to the same assumptions of heterosexual normality and superiority from their (heterosexual) feminist sisters as from the general population. They have suffered from the fears of heterosexual feminists that they and the movement might be labeled lesbian. Many lesbians have continued to fight for inclusion within the larger movement and to demonstrate the ways in which heterosexism and homophobia operate to divide women (Radicalesbians, 1971). At other times, this sense of alienation from the movement has led to separate organizing and the establishment of separate groups for lesbians as they seek to find safe space and community for themselves and attempt to build lesbian identification and analysis.

Other feminists have criticized the movement for its classist assumptions and for ignoring the voice and needs of working-class women and women assisted by the state (Stewart & Ostrove, 1993). Still others have criticized the growing division between academic feminists and community-based feminists, and between theory that is generated from the head and that which is grounded in the everyday experience of women. Academic feminists and other professionals are criticized for not being in touch with the real needs of everyday women. Professionals are sometimes viewed as having been co-opted by the system; in order to obtain the required credentials to be published, to teach in academia, or to practice counseling for fees, these women to some extent must adopt the patriarchal norms and expectations that are inherent in academic institutions and traditional disciplinary departments.

All these criticisms have been brought together through the analyses of feminists who support a social constructionist understanding of knowledge. Feminist social constructionists argue that our understandings of gender, race, class, and sexual orientation result in "real" material effects on people. The understandings of race and the stereotypes and prejudices we call racism result in material effects, deprivations and vulnerabilities, for people of color; our understandings of sexual orientation result in material effects for gays and lesbians that limit opportunities, rights, freedom, and power. The feminist project, from this perspective, is two-fold. First, we should work to challenge and change our societal constructions, our understandings of gender, race, class, and so on. Second, given the constructions we have, we can work to change the power structures in society so that certain groups of people are not systematically oppressed and denied opportunities. Feminists who appreciate the social constructionist perspective have generally been supportive both of multicultural notions of diversity and of efforts to understand and appreciate the diversity among women. At the same time, they seek ways to avoid divisiveness into smaller and smaller communities by building connections among diverse groups of women. The feminist project then becomes a task of establishing coalitions among women for political action (Mandel, 1994).

The Nature of Individual Women's Problems

A third debated issue is the question of how we account both for the problems that individual women experience and their responses to those problems. Radical feminists assert that women as a sex class are oppressed by the social and institutional systems of our culture. When women (or any group for that matter) are oppressed, individuals within the group develop ways of living with oppression on a daily basis. The responses of individuals in oppressed groups have been well documented. They often appear meek, passive, subservient. They learn what the oppressor wants and use that knowledge to satisfy some measure of their own wants and needs and sometimes seem to internalize the oppressor's view of them. Some may actually identify with the oppressor, trying to be as much like those in power as possible. In short, the more privileged group, the oppressor, ultimately both defines reality for and controls the resources of the oppressed group.

These are powerful mechanisms that result in certain predictable responses. But how are these responses to be understood? Are they simply behaviors that individuals use to survive and resist oppression? Or are they pathological behaviors induced by the experience of being oppressed? Within radical feminism, early in the second wave, a debate was begun between those who supported a "pro-woman line" (Hanisch, 1970) and those who supported a more psychological understanding of women's oppression. The pro-woman line promotes the notion that material conditions create women's oppression and determine women's behavior. A corollary of this view is that men oppress women for the economic benefits that accrue them by virtue of their privileged status as men. Proponents of the pro-woman line rejected all psychological explanations of women's behavior as false. They argued that women's behavior is not the result of brainwashing, stupidity, or mental illness. Rather, women act the way they do because it is their best means for resisting male dominance under oppressed conditions. The issue is power: Men have it, and women lack it.

Those who opposed the pro-woman line argued that it is sex-role conditioning that determines women's behavior (Koedt, 1970). From this perspective, men oppress women primarily for the psychological benefits of feeling powerful and in control, rather than for economic benefits. What women need to do, then, is "change their heads," deprogram themselves, raise their consciousness in order to realize they do not have to continue to be victims of their sex-role conditioning. The issue is sex roles: Women can conform or refuse to conform to these roles. The implications of these different understandings about women's responses to the problems they experience are particularly important to the development of a subversive counseling model. If a counselor believes that women are psychologically impaired by sex-role conditioning, she will focus on individual change—helping the woman reprogram her response to that conditioning, helping her heal from the effects of that conditioning. By contrast, if a counselor believes that women are always acting in their best interests in order to survive oppression, then women who come for counseling are viewed as able to see that their best interests may be served through collective political action.

Separatism and Alternative Systems

Another debated issue within radical feminism in the early 1970s was the question of separatism as a political strategy and the role and function of alternative systems. Many feminists had suggested that one of the strategies women might use, both to challenge male power and to refuse to conform to sex roles, is to refuse sex and marriage with men (Cronan, 1973; Firestone, 1970). Lesbian feminists, meanwhile, had been developing arguments to suggest that embracing lesbianism was the ultimate step in challenging male supremacy. Many feminists had already seen lesbianism as a natural extension of their feminist thinking, and radical lesbians offered a rationale for heterosexual feminists to define themselves as women-identified women (Radicalesbians, 1971). These kinds of analyses contributed to increasing the value of separatism as an important political strategy. Initially, separatism meant refusing to participate in the institutions of compulsive heterosexuality (Bunch, 1972; Rich, 1980) and marriage. But it soon came to be defined as physically separating from patriarchal society to establish women's communities where women could be safe and begin to define their own forms for building society. Hundreds of such communities, of varying size and geographical location, were established. Many still operate today, although we no longer hear much about a focus on developing new societal forms.

Other radical feminists viewed the establishment of alternative systems as a central part of both challenging and changing the existing social system. Examples of such alternative systems include women's health collectives, anti-rape programs, and battered women's shelters. These were viewed not only as places where women could come for help but also as alternative institutions developed to both challenge the legitimacy of the existing system and structure power differently. Like other leftist groups that promoted alternative institutions, however, these institutions over time began to be thought of as islands of safe haven outside the system, rather than as active political challenges to the system. This debate—this evolution or devolution of the function of alternative institutions—has relevance for battered women's programs today and for the kind of counseling models they promote. Are such programs challenging the system and structuring power differently? Or are the programs existing outside the system, providing services for women without fundamentally challenging the system? Also, have these programs been co-opted by the system, structuring themselves hierarchically and providing services for (nongendered) victims? Although these are organizational questions, they have implications for the kind of help being offered to battered women.

Organizational Structures

Related to the question of the role of alternative systems is the question of how power ought to be structured within feminist organizations. Early feminist groups, in an effort to eliminate the exercise of power and power hierarchies within their associations, attempted to create rules and principles to enforce equality.

Leaderless groups were initially attempted. These groups would often flounder when group goals and tasks were set, for no single person was responsible for ensuring who was supposed to do what. Jo Freeman, in an early article titled "The Tyranny of Structurelessness" (1972), points out that power and hierarchies in groups cannot be eliminated, though they may be unnamed and unacknowledged. The danger is that if no formal structures are articulated for a group, informal power can operate unchecked.

Because of the problems with attempts to eliminate leadership altogether, other groups decided to rotate leadership and other duties. Though some women were clearly better than others at some assignments, and better at some tasks than other tasks, the idea was that these duties—from making coffee to fund-raising to leadership—were skills that every individual could learn if given the opportunity.

For example, some women in a group might have been articulate and outspoken, but others were unable to express their ideas clearly and tended to be quiet. To respond to these differences, groups sought various methods to let the quiet women speak. Some tried to equalize time for each woman in the group to speak, but this approach created problems for women who did not want to talk about a particular issue. So, though these were admirable ideals in the abstract, in practice they often worked to create other kinds of inequities.

Because feminist groups were supposed to have no identifiable leaders, some women were subjected to severe criticism and occasionally ostracism when they were articulate, when they wanted to express their ideas within the group, or when they wrote for or spoke with the media. These criticisms became interwoven with ongoing feminist analyses of class issues, for class was another hierarchy that feminists sought to eliminate. So, women were criticized for "elitism" if they were perceived as seeking leadership within the group. Or they were criticized for "professionalism" if they had more education than others in the group and offered that background as a basis for leadership or ideas about group goals. These efforts to create and enforce complete equality led to a throttling of individual expression and a great deal of anger and hurt feelings (Echols, 1989).

Battered women's programs were not free from such conflicts. The question of the structure of power within an organization also has implications for the question of power between the woman who comes to an organization for help and the helper who works or volunteers for the organization—that is, it has implications for the nature of the relationship between client and counselor.

Consciousness-Raising

Another issue that arose within radical feminism was the role and aim of consciousness-raising (C-R) (Echols, 1989). Jaggar (1983) asserts that the overall political goal for radical feminists is a change in consciousness about the gendered ways in which we have viewed the world. Many individual women achieved this consciousness change through participating in the consciousness-raising groups that proliferated during the late 1960s and early 1970s. Once this change occurred, the world could never be seen or experienced in the same way, and a political strategy that emerged was the redescription of the new reality, that is, feminist analyses. However, a concern frequently expressed by some early radical feminist groups was that a focus on C-R often substituted for political action. These radical groups viewed the goal of C-R as building theory for concrete political actions. By contrast, there were those who argued that C-R is itself sufficient political action. From the latter perspective, C-R acts to transform the individual; the personal is political; therefore, C-R is a political act. C-R is frequently described as part of the process of feminist counseling, so the way in which C-R is viewed—whether it is viewed as an individual change that may (or may not) lead to political action or as a basis for directly discussing political action—has implications for a radical counseling model.

Each of these debated issues had an impact on the creation of feminist-defined feminist therapy approaches. Moreover, these issues continue to affect what we as feminist helpers do in our counseling today. Often we do not go back and think about these issues. We do not make conscious decisions about where we stand with regard to these debates or consider if our stance on one issue is consistent with our stance on another. However, we need to explicitly revisit these issues in our training of feminist practitioners, for our theoretical positions directly influence our counseling practices.

The Emergence of Feminist Therapy

Feminist therapy or feminist counseling began to develop as a distinctive approach to helping in the early 1970s. Naomi Weisstein (1971) charged that psychology had left women out by failing to include the social context in its theories, practices, and research. Phyllis Chesler's (1972) critique of the ways in which psychiatry and traditional therapy reinforce the oppression of women paved the way for alternative approaches to helping women. Initially, articles began appearing that discussed consciousness-raising groups as therapy for women (Brodsky, 1973; Kirsh, 1974). These were followed by works that specifically used the terms *feminism* and *feminist therapy* (Holroyd, 1976; M. Johnson, 1976; Lerman, 1976; Lindsey, 1974; Mander & Rush, 1974; Rawlings & Carter, 1977; Thomas, 1977) and defined the central characteristics of such therapy. The first decade of feminist therapy theorizing culminated in Sturdivant's *Therapy with Women: A Feminist Philosophy of Treatment* (1980) and Greenspan's *A New Approach to Women and Therapy* (1983).

Meanwhile, professional feminist psychologists organized the Association for Women in Psychology (AWP) in 1969, to act on psychology as a profession from outside the traditional structure of the American Psychological Association (APA). These women were acutely aware of APA's male-dominated structure. AWP lobbied APA for a division on the psychology of women and, in 1973, Division 35 was successfully established (AWP, 1991). Around this time, both grassroots feminist therapy collectives and professional feminist therapy institutes were being started by women in various communities around the nation. Also, grassroots feminist groups like battered women's shelters were beginning to offer counseling help to women.

The theoretical roots of feminist therapy are varied. There is no single source for a feminist theory of personality or therapy, and no set of specific feminist therapy techniques. Yet it is possible to describe some commonalities of feminist counseling, because there is a feminist philosophy of treatment that is based on a value system grounded in a political understanding of the oppression of women and the ways in which that oppression is materially and psychologically manifested (Sturdivant, 1980).

In describing their theories of counseling, many feminist therapists have identified what they believe are the essential components of feminist counseling. Ellyn Kaschak (1981) describes feminist therapy as differing from traditional therapy in its definitions of what constitutes healthy behavior for women, in its interpretations of the problems women clients present, and in its effort to decrease the power discrepancy between therapist and client. Faunce (1985a) adds that the feminist belief in the social and cultural roots of women's pain leads logically to a therapy in which both personal and social change are goals. Thomas (1977) reports that feminist therapists share a belief system comprised of feminist humanism and feminist consciousness. In addition, they value a nonhierarchical client-therapist relationship and employ consciousness-raising as a technique to emphasize women's common experiences. Thomas defines feminist humanism as a belief in the potential of women. She describes feminist consciousness as an awareness of the ways in which women's potential has been limited through stereotyped sex roles.

Gilbert (1980) defines two principles of feminist therapy. First, the personal is political. This principle develops out of an understanding of sex-role socialization and the ways in which women as a group are hurt by that socialization (similar to Thomas's feminist consciousness). It leads in therapy to a focus on validating the client's experience as a woman and, again, emphasizing change over adjustment. The second principle is that the therapist-client relationship is egalitarian. In therapy, this principle leads to the therapist demystifying the therapy process, being willing to self-disclose to the client, and modeling behaviors that are nontraditional for women, such as the expression of anger about women's, and the client's, experiences of oppression.

Hannah Lerman (1985) characterizes feminist therapy as emphasizing sexism as a primary contributor to women's pain. Therapy, then, must establish an egalitarian rather than hierarchical relationship. The therapist must respect the client's expertise about herself and her experiences and must be able to accept and interpret the client's negative feelings as a normal reaction to the oppressive condition of being a woman. Sandra Butler (1985) agrees, saying that feminist therapists must recognize that sexism and the real oppression of women create the conflicts, low self-esteem, and powerlessness of women who seek therapy. She urges the use of consciousness-raising as a therapeutic technique to assist clients in a cognitive restructuring of their beliefs about women. Consciousness-raising is best done in groups of women, according to Butler, but can also occur in the one-to-one relationship of therapist and client. She too stresses the need for an egalitarian therapist-client relationship and says that the therapist must identify with the goals and philosophy of feminism in order to promote social change for women.

Laidlaw and Malmo (1990) further describe the components of feminist therapy, emphasizing an equal (though not reciprocal) relationship between client and therapist. They affirm the value that women clients are the experts on their experience and that clients should have control of the therapy process. Clients must control not only the definition of the problem but also the setting of goals, making choices and implementing decisions, and the timing and pacing of therapy. Laidlaw and Malmo encourage the use of techniques to reach the client's nonrational understandings of experience. They also incorporate consciousness-raising as a way of reframing women's experience. They stress the importance of women's anger, the need for women to nurture themselves, and the value of women friends. Furthermore, they espouse the goal of client and social change, as opposed to client adjustment, and, like Faunce (1985a), recommend activating the client to participate in social change when she appears ready to do so.

Laura Brown (1994) argues for feminist therapy as a subversive dialogue. She analyzes the roots of women's personal distress as lying in our patriarchal societal structures. Women's behaviors, then, can serve as evidence of what is wrong in the social context but can also be interpreted as signs of survival that contain elements of protest and resistance to oppression. Women clients ultimately need liberation from the patriarchy, which can be accomplished only through social change. But they also need healing from the psychological internalization of patriarchy. Therapy must advance feminist resistance in clients, helping them refuse to accept dominant cultural norms. Therapy must also foster social change in the personal lives of clients and in their personal relationships with the social and political world. Brown's model of therapy supports political action over individual healing, though she adds that healing is likely to take place as well. She concurs that feminist therapy must take place in the context of an egalitarian relationship between client and counselor.

Despite different emphases, these depictions of feminist therapy have a number of themes in common. First, women's problems (for which they might seek help through counseling) are based in society—in women's oppression and in sex-role socialization. These factors result in both real material problems—structural barriers and limitations on personal choice— and internalized psychological problems, such as low self-esteem and feelings of powerlessness. Second, any improvement in the client's situation requires that the relationship between counselor and client be egalitarian, rather than recreating the hierarchical and oppressive power structures of the social system. Third, individual women need cognitive restructuring, or consciousness-raising, so they can understand how their personal pain is connected to sex-role socialization and the material oppression of all women. As individuals, women need real opportunities and options—housing, jobs, child care; as a group, women need political and social changes.

Feminist Therapy and Traditional Therapy

As the essential elements of feminist therapy were being defined during this historic period, there was often an effort to incorporate some elements of more traditional theories with feminist therapy. One of the central influences on feminist therapy was that of humanistic psychology (Faunce, 1985a; Sturdivant, 1980). In contrast to the seldom referenced radical therapy, the conceptual bases of humanism are common knowledge to most psychologists. Moreover, many of the tenets of humanistic psychology, such as the human potential for growth or self-actualization (Maslow, 1954, 1971), the importance of unconditional positive regard (cf. Rogers, 1961), and the emphasis on human choice, are familiar to and accepted by the popular culture. Humanism is considered the "third force" in psychology (psychoanalysis and behaviorism being the other two). According to Sturdivant, humanistic psychology contributed a client-centered approach to feminist counseling, acknowledging the client's expertise on her own experience, according client control of the counseling process, and positively valuing the client. In addition, feminist therapy incorporated humanism's growth-developmental model for individual women (Faunce, 1985a).

Although most feminist counselors employ humanistic concepts (Sturdivant, 1980), Muriel Greenspan (1983) has incisively identified the dangers in attempting to marry feminism and humanism. In the end, humanism fails women because it supports a highly individualistic approach to understanding psychological problems and entirely neglects the commonalities of women's problems as rooted in the social system. Furthermore, although affluent and middle-class women may be able to implement choices in the direction of personal growth, lower-class women face many more real barriers to such growth.

I agree with Greenspan's analysis. If the counselor accepts the humanistic ideas of client self-determination and personal growth as the sole basis for therapy, she will be ethically bound to a principle of noninterference in the client's life. Adherence to that principle will allow the therapist to be satisfied when the social roots of client problems are merely pointed out to the client, so there will rarely be an exploration of the necessity for clients to engage in social change. Moreover, the noninterference principle conflicts with the feminist acknowledgment of the value-laden nature of any therapeutic endeavor. For counseling to be truly subversive, to foster social change, it must give up its focus on trying to help individuals change their perceptions and instead encourage people to challenge the system that fosters their oppression.

As a way to resolve the inherent conflicts between humanism's emphasis on individual growth and feminism's emphasis on social change, some feminist therapists, despite their strong personal commitments to radical social change, have given up on the idea that psychology has any role to play in this endeavor. Rachel Perkins (1991), for example, has argued that psychology is totally incompatible with social change, because within therapy societal oppression becomes psychologized as an internalized pathological entity. Therapy then becomes limited to changing the internalized personal structures of oppression. I am not as pessimistic as Perkins, because I believe it is possible to merge individual change with social change if we develop an appropriate model and vigilantly maintain societal change as the focus. As Michelle Fine and Susan Gordon (1991) point out, feminist psychologists ought to perform their work in the space between the personal and the political, by connecting clients' personal experiences to collective movements of feminist politics.

In addition to humanism, other theoretical approaches to therapy have been attempted by some feminist counselors. For example, because much of the analysis of sex-role behaviors comes from social learning theory, the importance of therapist modeling has been stressed (Laidlaw & Malmo, 1990). Also, behaviorist techniques have been used in assertiveness training and the treatment of eating disorders and agoraphobia, which are predominantly problems for women clients (Blechman, 1980). However, some feminists have urged caution in the use of behavior techniques with women in the absence of an acknowledgment of women's oppression and vulnerability to male violence (Ellis & Nichols, 1979). Similarly, Fodor (1985) points out the dangers in providing assertiveness training to women when increased assertion can lead to increased violence from men attempting to maintain control. Such cautionary notes are particularly relevant to work with battered women.

Increasingly, professionally trained feminist therapists have attempted to integrate psychoanalytic theory with feminism (Dinnerstein, 1976; Prozan, 1992; Richardson & Johnson, 1984). Some contend that psychoanalysis is an appropriate method for understanding the effects of women's oppression on women's psychological development (Mitchell, 1974). Others have worked to free Freudian theory from its phallocentric bias by emphasizing the importance of the pre-oedipal relationship between mother and child (Chodorow, 1978; Eichenbaum & Orbach, 1983). More recently, some feminists have suggested that Lacanian psychoanalysis, the theories of the postmodernist Foucault, or both offer the best insights for understanding the experience of gender (Squire, 1989).

Both object relations theorists such as Chodorow and postmodernists represent a move away from the analysis of women's material oppression to a focus on understanding our psychological constructions of gender in specific social and historical contexts. Rigby-Weinberg (1986) provides a good summary criticism of feminist psychoanalytic and object relations theories. She contends that because such theories conceptualize women's distress as primarily intrapsychic, in the end they blame not only the victim-woman for her problems but also primary caretakers—mothers. In either event, they avoid placing responsibility on the social structure. Moreover, Rigby-Weinberg points out that feminist psychoanalysts still assume the role of expert (interpreting and analyzing resistance, transference, and the meaning of unconscious material) and therefore maintain a hierarchical therapist-client relationship.

Despite these differences in theory and the debates about the adequacy of each approach, the emergence of feminist therapies did much to improve the lot of women who came to therapy seeking help. However, the reliance on psychological constructs and the focus on the individual continued to work against a truly subversive and collective effort to radically change the social system.

Countersubversive Forces

Among the issues that obstructed the development of feminist counseling as a subversive activity were the concepts of healing and empowerment, ideas about the role of social change in counseling, and the ways in which each of these issues related to the nature of the therapeutic relationship and the role of the counselor.

The Concept of Healing

Notions of client distress and client pain lend themselves to metaphors of healing in the service of individual growth and development. Healing is frequently cited as a goal or outcome of feminist therapy. Although feminist counselors usually acknowledge the material bases of women's distress, most also consider the psychological effects of material oppression and tend to refer to those effects as pain, distress, or damage. Typically, this metaphor is used in the feminist counseling literature without question or meta-analysis. Laidlaw and Malmo (1990) are exceptions to this general rule. They elaborate on the concept of healing, citing its psychotherapeutic origins in the theories of Freud and Jung. They acknowledge that women have been hurt by their oppression within the social system and agree that the system must be changed. But they also believe that the individuals hurt by that system need psychological healing. They describe healing as a process that occurs from within the organism, even when the cause of the damage may be external. They believe that healing requires an intrapsychic resynthesis that usually involves a journey back to childhood. Faunce (1985b) also uses the metaphor of healing in describing the counselor's role as facilitating "the flow of helpful knowledge, energy, healing, and learning that comes from the client" (p. 315). Note that her description, like that of Laidlaw and Malmo, speaks of healing as coming from the client, in contrast to the medical model notion of healing as something an expert or physician does to or for a patient.

Unfortunately, notions like those cited above reinforce humanistic concepts of the individual as responsible for her situation, or at least for her reaction and perception of her situation, and for her own healing. I prefer Brown's (1994) idea of healing as a possible concomitant of feminist therapy rather than its central goal. This concept furthers the idea that if the oppressive social and political conditions were changed, women would be fine—they would be healed and future generations of women would not require this healing.

The Notion of Empowerment

Empowerment is another concept that is often cited as central in feminist theories of counseling. Smith and Siegel (1985) define empowerment as "the process of helping a powerless individual or group to gain the necessary skills, knowledge, or influence to acquire control over their own lives and begin to influence the lives of others" (p. 13). They suggest that people seek to have both personal power, the ability to determine one's life, and interpersonal power, the ability to influence others who have essential resources. They further contend that another form of empowerment is helping women gain awareness of the power they already have and the ways in which they have used that power.

Note that this conceptualization of empowerment is a very individualized notion. Smith and Siegel stop short of saying that women need political power as well. The empowerment strategy is simply seen as the counselor sharing or equalizing power with the client, and helping her become aware of her own existing power, so that the individual client gains a personal sense of self-efficacy.

The Role of Social Change in Counseling

A few feminist theorists state that it is important to involve the client in social change activities as part of the counseling effort (cf. Brown,

1994; Faunce, 1985a; Laidlaw & Malmo, 1990). However, most feminist theorists rely on the idea that consciousness-raising is a form of social activism, because it is an activity that connects personal experience with the awareness of women's common oppression in patriarchal society. Yet consciousness-raising by itself is little more than the process of insight that is supported by both psychoanalytic and humanist theories of therapy.

Those theorists who do suggest that social change activities should be part of counseling are seldom specific about the kinds of activities or the ways in which these should be incorporated. Nor do they offer an analysis of how the client might concretely benefit from such involvement. Brown (1994) is a notable exception, because she makes explicit the potential connection between social change activities and client healing. For the most part, however, a goal that ought to be a central feature of feminist counseling gets effectively dropped from the model that is held by most feminist counselors. The original emphasis on social change in and through counseling becomes transformed into an emphasis on the need for counselors to be involved in social change as part of their professional commitment.

Power in the Therapy Relationship

Questions of power and the sharing of power are central to the focus on the nature of the therapeutic relationship between client and counselor. Douglas (1985) provides a succinct review of the debate among feminist therapists about whether the client-therapist relationship should represent an effort toward equalizing power (Gannon, 1982), should be egalitarian in the sense that the two participants in therapy are equally valued, or should not involve power at all (Rohrbaugh, 1979). Adopting the model of social scientists French and Raven (1959), Douglas reviews the bases of power in feminist therapy. She concludes that feminist therapists have available to them and at times use each of six sources of power: reward, coercive, informational, expert, legitimate, and referent power. She believes, however, that feminist therapy can be defined by its emphasis on bilateral power strategies, on giving away power to the client, or empowerment of the client.

Rohrbaugh's idea that helping relationships between women should not involve any power parallels the idea that power should be equally distributed in feminist groups and organizations. But just as power discrepancies can never be eliminated in organizations, so too can they never be completely eliminated in the therapy relationship. The goal of feminist therapists, then, should be to articulate power, demystify the helping process, and encourage clients to define their needs, make decisions, and act. The feminist therapy relationship might be better viewed as one of temporary inequality (Douglas, 1985; Miller, 1976), which works toward a goal of sharing power and providing opportunities for clients to practice power.

The Role of the Counselor

The feminist belief in the centrality of an egalitarian relationship as a means for empowering the client has implications for the ways in which the role of the counselor is understood. Butler (1985) advocates adopting Ivey's psychoeducator model (1976) of the counselor, in which the counselor is thought of as a consultant and educator working with healthy persons attempting to solve or prevent problems. She points out the ways in which consciousness-raising as a technique results in cognitive restructuring (i.e., psychoeducation) around beliefs about women and self-as-woman. Chaplin (1988) refers to the feminist counselor as a container of client pain, a supporter of client decisions, and an enabler of client change. Laidlaw and Malmo (1990) view the feminist counselor as a guide, a friend, and a companion. They also urge counselors to act as advocates for the client and for social change. Finally, they stress the importance of counselors as models for their clients. Counselors not only model an alternative enactment of the role of woman but also model self-nurturance, expressions of anger about the social constraints on women, and their own valuing of women. Others have also cited the value of counselors serving as models (Gilbert, 1980; Lerman, 1985; Sturdivant, 1980).

Most of these potential counselor roles, including consultant, educator, container, supporter, enabler, guide, friend, model, and companion, support a humanistic counseling approach, in which the client is made responsible for her own changes. But, as noted earlier, it is necessary for the humanistic bases of feminist social change counseling to be re-evaluated and reconceptualized. This is not to argue that these are counselor roles that should never be enacted, but rather to suggest that other roles might be preferable when a counselor is focused on social change. The role of advocate begins to move in the direction of (social) action on the part of the counselor. However, for advocacy to work with a subversive counseling model, such action needs to include the client. Moreover, there are other counselor roles that will better assist the client in working to change oppressive conditions for all women.

As ideological refinements were being debated among feminist theorists, activists, and therapists, related issues specific to the efforts to help battered women were arising in the battered women's movement. And just as debated issues in feminism influenced the development of feminist therapy, so too did the special concerns of the battered women's movement relate to the refinements of counseling work with battered women.

The Radical Potential of
the Battered Women's Movement

Battered women's shelters originated as political action strategies of women who saw themselves working toward the liberation of women and the elimination of patriarchy by creating an alternative system for women (Burt, Gornick, & Pittman, 1984). The political aims of this alternative system were twofold. The ultimate goal was to eliminate violence against women, specifically battering in intimate relationships, but a corollary project was to develop new feminist forms of organizing and helping. As these autonomous programs for battered women began to network with one another, most eventually established formalized connections in state coalitions and with the National Coalition Against Domestic Violence (NCADV). Together, these programs and coalitions, battered women and helpers, make up the battered women's movement.

Several features of the battered women's movement contribute to its radical potential to transform society and, more specifically, to transform battered women into social activists. Susan Schechter (1982), using the Pennsylvania Coalition Against Domestic Violence (PCADV) to illustrate this potential, cites its radical commitments to feminist ideology, organization, and helping or counseling (see Appendix for background on PCADV). Moreover, PCADV contributed a program model (1987) to the movement that incorporates these commitments into six approaches that battered women's programs can strive to implement in their work within communities. A review and critique of each of these commitments can help you judge the relative success of the battered women's movement in achieving its potential.

Radical Purpose

The original aims of PCADV, as enumerated in its bylaws (PCADV, 1976a), are indeed remarkable in terms of their politically subversive stance. Not only was PCADV established to provide statewide services to victims of domestic violence, it was also intended "to eliminate domestic abuse of women and their dependent children in the Commonwealth of Pennsylvania . . . to expose the roots of domestic violence in the institutionalized subservience of women in this culture. . . . " Thus, in its original bylaws these radical goals—to eliminate violence caused by the institutionalized subservience of women—were established in a public document well before the advent of public funding. Though there are often concerns about the co-optative effect of government funding, PCADV has never modified the aims expressed in its bylaws, despite more than 15 years and millions of dollars in funding and grants from federal, state, and corporate sources. Its statement of purpose remains as radical today as it was in 1976. Consequently, counselors who work within the movement ought to assume a responsibility to keep that aim in mind: "to eliminate domestic abuse of women . . . to expose the roots of domestic violence."

Commitment to Diversity

PCADV's Principles of Unity (1976b) establish the philosophical commitment to include diverse groups of women:

We are women helping women deal with and overcome the oppressions we all face, i.e., sexism, racism, homophobia, classism, and ageism. We

support and encourage and will work for the participation of all women—
battered, women of color, lesbians, differently abled, older, and poor women.

This commitment translates politically to the establishment of caucuses
within PCADV: each representing a particular concern, each granted
political power to act, and each given a voice, with a commitment that
others will listen and try to understand. When NCADV was established 2
years later, it followed PCADV's lead and has, over the years, created
caucuses by and for women of color, lesbian women, older women, rural
women, and formerly battered women. These caucuses identify themselves as political units or groups of women who contribute analyses and
demands for particular needs of battered women as such needs are
modified by race, class, sexual orientation, age, and physical ability.

Neither PCADV nor NCADV has backed away from the potential
homophobia and racism of governmental or corporate funders by keeping
quiet about its constituencies. Internally, there have been heated debates
about these issues, accompanied by accusations of racism, homophobia,
heterosexism, ableism, elitism, and ageism against others in the movement. Though these conflicts are painful to everyone committed to ending
violence and oppression of women, they have also been the impetus for
personal and organizational growth and change to better respond to the
needs and concerns of all battered women. The endurance of the caucuses,
despite the conflicts, is an indication that women in this movement are
committed to the radical notion that the oppression of women is intimately
connected to other oppressions in society. The movement retains a focus
on anti-oppression work through its efforts to help battered women. Thus,
to understand and eradicate sexist oppression in all its forms, counselors
who work within the movement must incorporate ongoing self-monitor-
ing about personal "isms" while working with battered women.

Inclusion of Battered Women

The inclusion of battered women in PCADV and NCADV is a conscious attempt to recruit, include, involve, politicize, and empower the
victims the movement was established to help. Although battered women
as a group obviously span a broad political spectrum, PCADV and
NCADV believe it is important to pay close attention to formerly battered

women telling what they need from individual programs and the movement as a whole. The inclusion of battered women in the movement supports the principle that groups affected by a particular form of oppression can best define themselves and their needs and determine how to effect change. This principle stands in contrast to a colonization of battered women by which "experts" define the problem of domestic violence, develop methods for capitalizing on its victims, and promote individual adjustment or healing in ways that never challenge the roots of the problem. Moreover, the inclusion policies politicize battered women individually and collectively by building community and developing political goals.

Unfortunately, many programs have developed policies that exclude currently or recently battered women from participation. These policies were developed out of a concern that some battered women might be too close to their own experience of battering to effectively empathize and assist other battered women. That is, they might overidentify and assume that the circumstances of that woman's experience are the same as their own—and the decisions that woman makes should match those they have made. Such policies have been vociferously attacked by the caucuses of formerly battered women (McNees, 1994; Pence, cited in NiCarthy, 1988) and have never been publicly supported by PCADV or NCADV. Therefore, it remains the policy of the battered women's movement that counselors should eagerly look for ways to both include and join with their battered women clients as coworkers and activists against the social problem of woman battering.

Women Helping Women

Another distinguishing feature of the battered women's movement, articulated in the Principles of Unity quoted above, is the peer women-helping-women model, theoretically enhanced in the case of a formerly battered woman helping a battered woman. In contrast to the anti-rape movement (another radical feminist effort), PCADV and the battered women's movement as a whole have been successful in both maintaining the women-helping-women model and resisting the inclusion of male staff and volunteers. There are several factors that may contribute to this gender exclusivity. First, domestic violence was from the beginning defined as a crime of adult men against adult women. The battered women's movement never became subsumed by a focus on male victims or on the abuse of children. Although it was recognized that a batterer might also physically or sexually abuse the children in the household, in the early days PCADV and NCADV believed that the responsibility for protecting the children should be left with the mother or the state agencies created for that purpose.[1] Mothers found to physically abuse their children were offered, in shelters, nonviolent alternatives to that kind of parenting and were shown how their violence toward children paralleled the batterer's violence toward them. Second, battered women's programs in most states were never seduced, by the advent of crime victims funding, into changing their focus from domestic violence to general crime victims services. Although crime victims funding was sometimes accepted, it was used for crime victims of domestic violence, not to extend services to victims of other crimes. So there was never a strong affiliation between the battered women's movement and the more conservative and gender-neutral National Organization of Victim Assistance. The directors of battered women's centers never thought of woman battering as a subset of crime victimization.

The women-helping-women model is potentially radical on several levels. First, it rejects male help and simultaneously rejects the notion of men as experts and authorities on women and rescuers and protectors of them. Second, the model views women as the experts on their own experience and as competent to help other women, and it promotes and models equality in relationships. Other helping models, particularly those in which men are helping women or those that follow a medical model, reinforce the cultural icons of men as experts and protectors and women as incompetent and helpless; thus, they recreate relationships of inequality.

Battering of Men

One potential threat to the women-helping-women model is the problem of battering in gay male relationships, particularly when a gay man seeks help from a domestic violence program. Although the phenomenon of gay male battering has been acknowledged, it never became a focus in the battered women's movement. Also, almost every battered women's program has encountered the occasional man who claims to be abused by a woman. Often programs deal with men's requests for services by referring them elsewhere. The rationale is that the battered women's movement and its programs are for battered women, not men. Although the movement might not go so far as to state that women never physically abuse men in intimate relationships, it insists that the principal element of the social problem that is named "domestic violence" is that of men battering women. Many of those involved in the movement assume that if men beat each other up, that is a problem for which men should be responsible. Although counseling services to battered men—gay or straight—have sometimes been offered when requested, shelter services have not. So there has never been an influx of male victims in battered women's programs, and the women-helping-women model has remained intact.

Battering in Lesbian Relationships

Recently, attention has been directed toward the issue of battering in lesbian relationships. Although this issue does not directly threaten the women-helping-women model, it has been a difficult problem for feminists to acknowledge and analyze, because it does threaten a gender-specific analysis of battering in which men and the patriarchy are viewed as the perpetrators of violence against women (Kelly, 1986). The ideal of cultural feminists and others who rely on determinist explanations of behavior is that women are nonviolent and would never aggress against or intentionally hurt another person, particularly another woman. So when a woman does batter another woman, we must look for ways to explain this aberration. It is all too easy for heterosexuals to "explain" lesbian women who batter by focusing on the issues related to sexual orientation.

Part of the difficulty is that the power imbalance in a lesbian battering situation is not a social given as it is in heterosexual relationships, so it is necessary to resort to psychological concepts about sex-role socialization and the internalization of patriarchal values in some lesbians. Unfortunately, some of the interpretations offered reinforce stereotypes about lesbian relationships. Important efforts have been made to address the issues in lesbian battering from the perspective of those who have been victims (Lobel, 1986; NCADV, 1994; Pharr, 1989). These authors look for the social roots of lesbian battering in the homophobia and heterosexist assumptions of our culture and analyze the connection of these forms of oppression to other forms of oppression, including racism and sexism. They suggest that battered women's programs often have difficulty dealing with battered lesbians because of the homophobia of workers in the program.

Therefore, if battered women's programs are successful in fighting their own homophobia, the women-helping-women model can remain successfully intact in working with battered lesbians (Pharr, 1989).

Occasionally there have been programmatic difficulties when both partners in a lesbian relationship seek help, as victims, from the same program. Because the basic stance of these programs is to *believe the victim,* and because many programs have policies about not offering services to batterers, these two positions may be in conflict with each other in such cases. In an effort to deal with the dilemma about who to believe in these cases, NCADV has taken a strong position about lesbians who batter not being welcome. Indeed, at the most recent national conference, there were statements in the conference program about ensuring the safety of battered lesbians by excluding batterers from participation.

Nonhierarchical Organizational Model

The first battered women's centers, like the first women's centers and rape crisis centers, were committed to a collective, nonhierarchical organizational model as an antidote to traditional family and institutional structures. Indeed, the nature of shelter work is that women—both battered women and volunteer or staff women who are helping—are living and working together in a household. That collective style of living and working together is therefore a process of the effort to help in a much more extensive way than it can be in other types of women's self-help programs, such as rape crisis centers.

Certainly, this feature of the battered women's movement had the potential for maintaining an organizational commitment to nonhierarchical structures. Still, other factors were operating to obviate that commitment, forcing most battered women's programs in the United States to structure themselves in more traditional ways. One of these factors is the requirement of most funding sources that programs be incorporated as legal entities, so that there is some assurance of fiscal accountability. Legal requirements and funders' mandates for nonprofit status and volunteer boards of directors begin to create hierarchical structures, for they tend to focus responsibility and authority in some identified positions. In addition, when organizations are required to set up boards of directors, they face the dilemma of either seeking broad-based community support or sticking to rigid standards of feminist principle. The first option runs the risk of so modifying the program that it no longer seeks radical social change and instead turns its focus to providing quality services. The second option may limit community acceptance and affect community perception of the program, thus interfering with its ability to reach out to many battered women. In Pennsylvania, largely due to the support and example of PCADV as an organization, most local programs have successfully achieved a fair balance between community acceptance and feminist activist goals and have maintained their identity as feminist programs. But there is no denying that compromises of various sorts are also made.

Perhaps a more fundamental problem occurs when an organization grows from a grassroots volunteer effort to an agency in which at least some staff are paid (Riger, 1994). Even in small programs with only one or two paid staff members, a distinction has been created between volunteers and staff. That distinction is reflected not only in salaried status but also in the differentiation of tasks and responsibilities. As the number of paid staff increases, so too does the differentiation of tasks and, almost inevitably, an increasing differentiation of salaries, based on levels of responsibility, years of experience, and sometimes educational level. These organizational features necessarily preclude a full commitment to nonhierarchical, collective work. In Pennsylvania, battered women's shelters are organized legally in traditional ways. They are incorporated as nonprofit agencies, with a volunteer board of directors that hires an executive director who then hires the staff and is responsible for the operation of the program. Although efforts may be made to minimize salary differences between workers who answer the phone and maintain the paperwork and those who "direct" the program and report to boards of directors, or between workers who were recently hired and those who have been with the program for 10 years, or between workers who contribute a great deal of time and effort and those who contribute a minimum amount of time and effort, there are few programs that take the total pool of money for salaries and divide it evenly among all staff. Internally and informally, there may be some modifications of the traditional structure. For example, there may be individual organizational commitments to some of the forms of collectivity, such as consensus decision making. But the reality is that the power and control of each of the programs in Pennsylvania lie with the board of directors, the executive director, or both.

It is important to explicate the issues of hierarchy in organizational structures because these issues have a carryover into the program's approaches to helping, affecting the radical potential of collective, non-hierarchical organizations. If collectivity, equality, nonspecialization, and feelings of sisterhood or "communitas" characterize those who work together in programs, then those feelings, attitudes, postures, and ways of working are more likely to carry over into the helping relationship. The counselor's relationship with the battered woman who comes for help is more likely to be characterized by equality, a sense of peerness, mutual identification as women, and commitments to work together on the problems at hand.

Still, despite the compromises and the inevitable creation of some forms of hierarchy as organizations grow, the battered women's movement has been more successful than the anti-rape movement at maintaining a philosophical commitment to some forms of collectivity and consensus decision making. However, as Gornick, Burt, and Pittman (1983) point out, maintaining a collective work structure does not guarantee a feminist philosophy and social change emphasis within a center. Moreover, Michelle Fine (1985) notes how the social visions of socialist feminists are often at vari- ance with the goals advocated for individual battered women. For example, she points out how the social vision encourages shelters organized around collectivity, interdependence, and shared resources, but the individual goals for battered women encourage autonomy, independence, and self-sufficiency. In making this observation, Fine foreshadows one of the central findings of my research and one of my primary concerns about counseling practice with battered women.

Empowerment Counseling

Another component of the radical potential of the battered women's movement is its counseling model. In Pennsylvania, PCADV uses the word *empowerment* in public documents, such as program standards, and specifically refers to empowerment counseling in training manuals. The definition offered by PCADV for empowerment counseling reads,

> Empowerment counseling is a wellness-based helping method in which battered women become increasingly able to take control of their lives. The philosophical basis of empowerment counseling assumes that victim/sur-

vivors of battering can determine what is best for their lives if they are offered support, advocacy, resources and information. As the helper and victim/survivor affirm the equality of their power, the competence of battered women is affirmed. Battered women become able to acknowledge their own power and authority to act. Empowerment counseling includes consciousness-raising as a method which creates a shared understanding of the ways in which sexism is institutionalized, pervading every aspect of our lives. This understanding may elicit anger about the social climate which fosters abuse, but it also creates a shared appreciation of women's experience and women's unique strengths. The goal of empowerment counseling is not only to return control to victim/survivors, but to involve survivors in assisting other battered women and building a collective strength among all women. (PCADV, 1987, glossary [pages not numbered])

Like many definitions, this one is dense, packed with multiple meanings. It is based in radical feminist commitments and shares features with many of the components of feminist therapy. As one of the authors who provided the initial conceptual framework and language of the empowerment counseling definition, I am in a good position to "unpack" some of the intended meanings, to compare and contrast those commitments with traditional, nonfeminist counseling methods, and to clarify some of the ways in which ideas about empowerment can be modified by the goals of radical social change.

A Wellness Approach

First, we note that this is a *wellness-based* approach. That is, the counselor or helper is expected to approach battered women with respect for their success in surviving. Battered women are not to be viewed as psychologically impaired or damaged or as wanting to be battered. Rather, battered women are acting as best they can to resist and survive violence and oppression. By contrast, traditional therapists often approach those who seek counseling services from a medical model perspective that features diagnoses of psychopathology and analysis of unconscious resistance to change.

Self-Determination

Second, this is an approach based on the principles of individual choice and *self-determination*. Neither individual counselors nor the battered women's movement can know either what will work best for any individual battered woman or what she is capable of doing at any particular time. Battered women need support, material resources, and information so that they can make decisions that will best serve their interests, given the available options and potential risks. Although these principles are similar to those held by most humanist counselors, they are modified by acknowledgment of the material realities of women's oppression and the real dangers and economic deprivation facing battered women.

Counselor Role

Third, the role of the counselor is to *provide support, identify resources, supply information,* and at times *serve as an advocate* for the battered woman. By contrast, the role of traditional counselors and therapists is to diagnose, analyze, and interpret the underlying meanings, behavioral effects, or both, of the client's verbalizations and behaviors in therapy and in her personal life and relationships.

Counseling Relationship

Fourth, the relationship between the counselor and client should be characterized by *affirmations of equality of power.* The counselor's actions should demystify the notion that she is the expert and affirm the battered woman's authority and competence to make decisions and act. Counselor and battered woman talk and work together to solve a problem. This feature of the empowerment counseling definition tends to ignore or minimize the inherent power imbalance in a relationship in which one party is seeking help and the other is hoping to provide help. It stands in contrast to traditional therapies that operate out of a hierarchical structuring of power, often unarticulated, in which the therapist knows best, understands more, and directs the counseling process.

Techniques of Counseling

Fifth, the techniques of counseling include the *fostering of women's anger,* the *identification of battered women with other women* (particularly other battered women), and *consciousness-raising* about institutionalized sexism. In contrast, traditional therapists have often worked to soften or

"resolve" women's anger, have made no effort to foster women's identification as a sex class, and have effectively isolated battered women by
interpreting their problems as individual aberrations that can be modified
if women change their attitudes, their behaviors, their relationships, or
all three. Instead of consciousness-raising, traditional therapists have
worked to analyze the unconscious psychosexual structures, or behaviors,
or both of individual women that maintain a sense of self-identity. Their
idea is that self-understanding, or behavior change, or both may lead to
changes in the experience of battering.

Goal of Counseling

Finally, the stated goal of this definition of empowerment counseling
is *to involve battered women in a collective effort to help other battered
women.* The implied goal is to involve battered women in the battered
women's movement. By contrast, the goal of traditional therapists is to
work toward a solution or resolution of the individual woman's presented
problem.

Criticisms and Challenges:
The Nexus of Theory and Practice

The general features of the battered women's movement that contribute
to its radical potential—its radical purpose, its attention to racial, class,
and sexual diversity; its inclusion of battered women; its models for
organizing and helping—also create the basis for ideas, structures, and
processes that at times operate to subvert that potential.

The Bias Against Professionals

Among the ideas that act to counter the radical potential of the
movement are the conceptual dichotomization of battered women and
professionals and the anti-professionalism bias of the movement. Susan
Schechter (1988) warns feminist movements against the "pitfall" of professionalism, that is, becoming increasingly dependent on professionally
trained women to provide services. Though I tend to agree with much of
Schechter's analysis, on this particular point we part company (Schechter,

1988; Whalen, 1988). This aversion to professionalism is particularly relevant to the issue of counseling battered women, because in attempting to empower battered women as counselors, it may simultaneously disempower radical feminists who are professionally trained.

The anti-professionalist stance certainly had its merits in the 1970s. Traditional professional approaches prior to this period had typically encouraged the battered woman to stay in her marriage (or to get married if she wasn't) and try harder to be a good wife. If it became obvious that this tactic was ineffective in stopping the abuse, women were hospitalized, tranquilized, or medicated for depression. Radical feminists deplored the helping professions—psychiatry, psychology, counseling, social work, and nursing—for trying to help battered women adjust to and accept their ongoing physical abuse. For radical feminists, the answer was to challenge the sanctity of the institution of marriage and the goals of professional helpers, and to encourage battered women to get out of their abusive relationships and get free. Battered women's programs were established to offer feminist alternatives to the traditional approach, so there was a built-in antipathy to the professional tactics for helping battered women that had been operative prior to the establishment of the movement. Battered women's programs and shelters conceptualized their alternative as a peer, self-help approach for battered women, using a women-helping-women model. Battered women were viewed as best able to help other battered women.

Within the helping professions in the 1970s, feminists were only beginning to concur with the analysis that psychology and therapeutic approaches had failed all women, and battered women in particular. Therefore, feminist professionals were only in the early stages of developing their own analyses of how a specifically feminist approach to counseling might be used to raise the consciousness of battered women so that they could leave abusive relationships. But since the 1970s, there have been substantial contributions to this analysis and work from feminists within the helping professions. Yet despite the growth of feminist approaches to counseling, the battered women's movement has strenuously continued its anti-professional stance (Battered/Formerly Battered Women's Task Force, 1992) and in doing so has denied the veracity of its own helping efforts by creating a false dichotomy between professionals and battered women in the movement.

First, let us consider what the battered women's movement means in 1995 by "helping." I use the word *helping* because there often is a strong reluctance to call this activity *counseling*. The ideal is that battered women come to programs to talk to other battered women, as peers, about strategies to get free and stay safe. Battered women helpers are offering information about resources and options and are sometimes offering to serve as advocates for the woman as she seeks legal recourse. In actuality, the people, either volunteering or hired to fulfill this role of talking with the battered women who come to the program for help, are frequently not formerly battered women. Moreover, the skills sought in these program workers and the skills offered through required training programs for volunteers and workers are those of listening and responding in an empathic, nonjudgmental, supportive manner. Workers are not only trained to practice empathic listening and supportive responding but are also encouraged to be nondirective (in terms of telling the woman what she ought to do), to validate the woman's experience, to refuse to blame the woman in any way for any of her experiences. So, despite the reluctance to call this listening and responding activity counseling, that is in fact what it is. The basic programmatic need is for counselors. A formerly battered woman may or may not have the necessary skills to work as a counselor (McNees, 1994), to listen to the experience of a woman in crisis and pain, to help her understand the options available to her now and in the future, and to allow her to make decisions about her life that the counselor believes might endanger her further.

A conceptual dichotomy between battered women, as a group, and professionals, as a group, is simply not tenable. After all, professionals—women trained and educated in psychology and counseling—can also be battered. Thus, the effort to exclude professionals may end up excluding and disempowering some battered women. On the other hand, not all women—battered or not—are able to provide the necessary empathic, nonjudgmental listening and responding skills to effectively help another battered woman. Consequently, insisting that only battered women should be part of the movement could result in other battered women not getting the help they need and want. If a dichotomy is to be drawn in trying to define who best can help battered women, it might be a dichotomy between women with counseling skills who hold radical feminist ideals about the battered women's movement and those who do not. Then, those who had counseling experience and training would not automatically be negatively labeled as professionals. Rather, they could be assessed for their understanding of and commitment to the ideology and goals of the movement. Conversely, there would be no automatic assumption that a formerly battered woman would a good counselor or that she would have taken on the ideology of the movement simply because she has been battered. The latter assumption is just as dangerous as the former.

The reality is that battered women's programs typically look for workers with some kind of counseling experience or background, sometimes establishing educational requirements, often advertising the job as "counselor wanted." Moreover, formerly battered women are often given priority consideration for the counseling jobs in battered women's programs. That is, when a program has two women with the requisite skills and training to work as a counselor or advocate, it may well prefer to hire the one who has also survived a battering relationship. This preference is in keeping with the movement's commitments to helping and empowering battered women. My point, however, is this: For the most part, programs are looking for workers with good counseling skills who are also committed to the ideology and goals of the battered women's movement. Unfortunately, NCADV even today continues its public anti-professionalism stance (Fields & Conrey, 1994).

There is another concern with this anti-professionalism stance. It could disempower battered women by discouraging them from getting a higher education. A stated goal of the battered women's movement is to provide training and experience to battered women who might not have had such opportunities. But that goal may be in conflict with NCADV's anti-professionalism stance. How can we encourage individual battered women to better themselves economically and enhance their sense of personal power if we tell them not to go to college, not to take psychology courses, not to get degrees and certifications, not to become professionals? How can we build a movement that, through its helping activities, promotes the politicization of battered women if we do not educate women about both the radical feminist ideologies that foster social change goals and the radical feminist counseling approaches that make explicit the connection between ideology and practice?

This challenge to NCADV's anti-professionalism stance and the questions raised about the nature of its helping-counseling activities is not meant as a challenge to the ideology of the battered women's movement.

In fact, the basic ideology has considerable merit, and our counseling models need to better reflect that ideology. In short, the ideology is based in the belief that woman battering is a social problem of violence against women by men. Woman battering is enabled by the institutional arrangements of marriage and the family, by sex-role conditioning, and by societal abuse of power and domination in the forms of sexism, racism, classism, homophobia, ableism, ageism, and other oppressions. The answer to the problem of violence against women lies in radical social change of our society and its institutions. In helping and counseling battered women, we ought to be politicizing women to take power and change society.

The Notion of Empowerment

Another development that has inadvertently subverted the movement's radical potential is the distortion of the notion of empowerment. When Paolo Freire initially developed his ideas about empowerment (1970), the concept was based on notions of empowerment and emancipation of the people, as a group, so that they could seize freedom from their oppressors. Liberation pedagogy was the method developed to achieve the requisite consciousness change, to practice power in the "classroom," and to develop strategies for change outside that classroom. It was in keeping with this conception of empowerment that PCADV chose the name for its counseling model. But psychologists, certainly by training and perhaps by our own inclinations, are so prone to think not only individually but also acontextually and ahistorically that we have transformed the original notion of group empowerment into one of individual empowerment, characterized by increased *feelings* of personal strength, decision-making ability, and self-efficacy. Such feelings may or may not be connected to behavioral change and are rarely capable of altering the material circumstances of most individuals. The primary problem with the notion of individual empowerment is that it shifts the locus of responsibility, the identified source of problems, from the social and material to the individual. From there, it is only a small step from making the assumption of personal responsibility to developing therapeutic goals directed at "healing" through cognitive change: Change your head, and the world will look better to you. Although that change might work well enough for one individual, it will never alter the social reality that women are oppressed and women are beaten by men as one means of controlling them.

Another of my conceptual difficulties with the strategy of client empowerment comes from the denotative aspects of the word itself. *To empower* means to grant power to another. As Stephanie Riger (1994) notes, there is a fundamental paradox in the idea of empowerment. It presumes an agent who is granting the power—the therapist—and a subject who is given the power—the client (Gore, 1992). One has to question these assumptions on several levels. First, the concept is in conflict with the notion of an egalitarian relationship between counselor and client. I am not, however, as concerned with the acknowledgment that the counselor-client relationship can never be an equal one as I am about the idea that a woman counselor can be presumed to have power to give away. After all, as a woman, she is subject to the same forms of oppression that other women experience. I am unclear how the disempowered can empower others who are also disempowered. What we can do as feminist therapists, however, is explicate power, talk with the client about how power operates and what its effects are, engage the client in developing power strategies, and join with the client in seizing political power. By these means, we can replace the notion of individual empowerment with concepts of the power of *women as a group* to effect social change.

The Inconsistency of Practice and Theory

Both of the issues discussed above are semantic and ideological constructions that can be refigured, redefined, or renamed to better fit the challenges of the movement and the needs of battered women as we approach the 21st century. But a more fundamental problem confronts both the battered women's movement and feminist practitioners in the counseling professions, which is that our practice is often inconsistent with our ideological goals for transforming society and creating a world in which violence against women no longer exists. We operate from one model for helping individuals, and another for reforming or changing society. More often, we have given little or no thought to the specific questions about the existence of male violence against women, the ideal society, and the means for achieving our vision. Our approaches to helping battered women—whether developed out of professional clinical experience or grassroots experience in shelters—remain disconnected in essential ways from our understandings of the social problem of woman battering. In the following chapter, I will review specific approaches and theories developed by feminists to work with battered women. In some cases, the theories are characterized by an approach that is too individual, so the practice of helping battered women is inconsistent with a feminist analysis of the social problem of woman battering. In other cases, the theories are infused with the radical feminist analysis, but we must question how and whether those theories are implemented in counseling practice with battered women.

Note

1. Over the past 15 years, there has been a growing move in the battered women's movement to advocate for children as a group with their own needs and interests, which may at times conflict with the needs and interests of their battered mothers. Many programs have hired "children's advocates" and there is now a Child Advocate caucus within NCADV.

5

Counseling Practice
With Battered Women

Thus far, I have expressed doubts about whether the radical potential of feminist therapy is always realized, particularly when our models for helping become overly individualized and psychologized. I have also questioned the consistency of the battered women's movement, which, though radical in its ideology, might not put its radical theories to work in its counseling practices. To complete my articulation of why it is important for a new counseling model to be adopted, I will focus here on the feminist counseling theories and models that have been specifically developed for helping battered women. In the following pages, the work of both *professional* feminist counselors and *grassroots* feminist counselors will be compared and contrasted, for these shed light on the ways in which our ideas about social change for women often fail to translate into our counseling practices.

Feminist Analyses
of Woman Battering

Feminist analyses of the social problem of woman battering suggest that violence occurs because of cultural beliefs about sex roles and the institutional arrangements that result from these beliefs, especially marriage and the traditional patriarchal family. In the traditional family, as characterized in feminist literature, the man is culturally granted the authority to lead, direct, make decisions for, and control his wife and children. The man is the king of his castle, the head of his household. Historically, laws concerning the property, conjugal, and disciplinary rights of men have supported this family structure (Brownmiller, 1975; Martin, 1976). Violence or the threat of violence is one of the more powerful and effective means for a man to maintain control in his family.

The woman victim of such violence is viewed, in this feminist analysis, as doing the best she can to survive in her situation. Therefore, the earliest feminist works on battering (Martin, 1976; Warrior, 1976) de-emphasized the psychological state of the victim. Rather, the battered woman was viewed as a psychologically healthy woman who needed resources in order to leave her batterer. Specifically, she needed a safe place to go with her children, information about the options available to her, and time to think and develop a plan for leaving and surviving on her own. These authors suggest that the only reasons women stay in or return to abusive relationships are fear of further abuse, beliefs about the value of keeping the family together, and economic realities.

Even in these analyses, however, the battered woman's psychological state is not completely ignored. Martin (1976), in particular, intersperses her primarily social analysis with references to battered women's lack of self-worth, self-confidence, and motivation to change, and their sense of shame and despair. She proposes strategies for combating these psychological problems, including feminist psychotherapy, consciousness-raising groups, and, for some women, assertiveness training. The goal of these efforts should be to have the woman "regain a sense of her own identity and individuality as a person" (Martin, p. 153).

Lenore Walker and
Her Critics and Disciples

Several years after Martin's and Warrior's publications, a few feminist professional psychologists began writing about battered women. Chief among these was Lenore Walker, whose extensive work on battered women has spanned more than 15 years. Within the profession of psychology, she has become the most widely recognized expert in domestic violence. She describes herself as a feminist and grounds her analysis of violence against women in feminist theory (1989a). Her research looks at the psychological effects on women of chronic episodic violence in a relationship; however, her work has been challenged by grassroots feminists who claim that her theories are not descriptive of the experience of most battered women (Pence & Shepard, 1988; Warrior, 1985). In addition, her theories have been criticized as victim-blaming (Gondolf, 1988) and preserving the prerogatives of male supremacy (Warrior). Walker's decision to testify for the defense in the case of Nicole Brown's murder has drawn sharp criticism from the battered women's movement and has raised serious questions even among her feminist colleagues in psychology. Despite these criticisms, it must be recognized that Walker has made an immense contribution to psychology and to the battered women's movement by challenging traditional notions of battered women (1979), by promoting public policies that support battered women (1984a), and by advocating on behalf of battered women accused of murdering their abusers (1989b). In fact, I have personally reviewed most of the feminist psychological literature that pertains to battered women and have seldom come across ideas, theories, or applications that diverge significantly from those offered by Walker. For the most part, a review of Walker's work encompasses a review of the extant feminist psychological theories on woman battering (cf. Dutton, 1992; Herman, 1992).

Walker has relied heavily on psychological theory for most of her explanations about the effects of battering on women. In particular, she has drawn upon the model of learned helplessness (Seligman, 1975), to help explain why battered women stay in abusive relationships. Walker writes,

> They learn that their voluntary responses really don't make that much difference in what happens to them. . . . It becomes extraordinarily difficult for such women . . . to believe their competent actions can change their life

situation. Like Seligman's dogs, they need to be shown the way out
repeatedly before change is possible. (Walker, 1977, pp. 526-527)

For a battered woman to change her learned helplessness responses, she
first must be persuaded to leave the battering relationship. Shelters and
safe houses are helpful here. Second, the woman needs to learn to reverse
her negative cognitive set about the effectiveness of her competent actions
and to begin taking control of her life. Therapy to promote self-esteem
and relieve depression can help "erase . . . victim potential" (Walker,
1979, p. 54). It is in phrases like the latter that grassroots feminists base
some of their more vehement objections to Walker's theories.

Emerging from Walker's work is the cycle theory of violence, which
identifies some of the behavioral reinforcements the battered woman
receives that perpetuate her remaining in the relationship. Rooted in a
tension reduction hypothesis, the theory describes three phases of the
battering relationship. In the tension-building phase, the woman may try
to avoid abuse through efforts to please. In the explosion phase the
battering incident occurs, and it is the batterer who has control over when
he will stop. The third phase of the cycle is the contrition phase in which
the batterer becomes loving and apologetic. It is this phase that provides
the affectional rewards women seek from marriage. The woman hopes that
this phase can be maintained and that the other phases will not recur. Over
time, Walker writes, "She becomes an accomplice to her own battering"
(1979, p. 69) by continually seeking the third phase. The contrition phase
gradually becomes shorter and shorter, however, and may eventually
change to a phase of no tension, without overt expressions of love or
contrition. In order for women to break this cycle of violence, they must
first become aware of the pattern. This analysis, too, has been challenged
by grassroots feminists, who react strongly to the notion that a battered
woman can exercise any control over the battering or that she would ever
be an accomplice.

A variety of treatment approaches and modalities for working with
battered women are considered by Walker (1980). Psychodynamic and
other insight-oriented models are criticized as inappropriate for battered
women. These models, based in beliefs about the innate nature of aggression, encourage victims and aggressors to discharge aggression periodi-
cally in smaller doses and in safer ways so that aggression does not build
to the point of explosion; however, they ignore the ongoing aspects of

power and control in male-female intimate relationships and in effect deny the benefits that accrue to the man for his aggressive displays. Walker puts somewhat more trust in social learning approaches that understand aggression as learned behavior. These models teach anger management techniques that have proved useful to some couples but again ignore issues of power and control.

Generally, Walker (1980) believes that the grassroots shelter system has been most effective in helping battered women. Shelters use a paraprofessional and peer counseling model rooted in crisis intervention philosophy. Crisis intervention is particularly appropriate after an acute battering incident, when most women seek shelter, for it allows a focus on a specific critical incident, assessing the potential for lethality. In addition, plans can be made for present and future safety while information is provided about legal options and community resources. Yet crisis intervention or sheltering does not interrupt the cycle of violence or lead to lasting changes. Usually, the only way to end violence in a violent relationship is to end the relationship. Walker concludes her overview of crisis intervention with battered women by stating, "Although some battered women are ready to use crisis therapy to help them separate permanently, most need more time" (1980, p. 354).

Walker (1980) next turns to a review of treatment modalities, including individual, group, and couples therapy. Like most grassroots feminists, she rejects couples therapy in violent relationships because battered women can never be free from intimidation and therefore cannot participate in the counseling situation freely, equally, and without fear of reprisal. The most helpful treatment modality for battered women is individual psychotherapy that has as its goal increased independence. Therapy should concentrate on the present, although it may use the past to promote understanding of the current situation. Therapy should be action-oriented rather than analytical. It must include a career or vocational planning component and it must involve cognitive restructuring if changes are to be permanent. Walker does not, in this text, specify the beliefs that need to be restructured.

Group therapy, if it is done in groups composed of other battered women, is also highly recommended by Walker (1980). A group can reduce the sense of isolation felt by the battered woman. She can learn new cognitions from others in the group. and she can benefit from the group norms that support positive behavioral change. Walker believes that the positive effects of group therapy for battered women may help explain the success of shelters that operate with either specific group formats or informal group structures involved in living together with other battered women. Groups should be roughly divided into two stages. The first stage would be for battered women in crisis or trying to get free from the relationship. NiCarthy's (1984) guide for battered women's groups covers this first stage. The second stage would be for women who have been successful at getting out of the relationship and are now facing other developmental life issues, such as establishing new intimate relationships.

Therapeutic interventions with battered women are difficult, Walker believes, because of "the need battered women have to manipulate everyone in their environment" (Walker, 1984b, p. 126). This manipulative behavior derives from the hypervigilance a battered woman must maintain to help her avoid further abuse. The therapist must help the woman discuss the details of her abuse so that both the therapist and the woman come to realistically assess the danger. Walker suggests using guided imagery to help the woman imagine more assertive behaviors on her part and fantasize different outcomes to the tension-building stage. This process promotes the building of self-esteem in a battered woman by supporting her existing strengths and helping her reevaluate her self-worth and competence. These techniques result in cognitive restructuring, which can broaden the choices a battered woman may have. Finally, Walker advocates "allowing the woman to regain her own power in the therapy relationship" (1984b, p. 127) so that she may reexperience power in other relationships in her life.

Another major concern for battered women centers on the coercive techniques employed in violent relationships. Walker (1979, 1994) offers the conceptualization of a battered woman's syndrome that may be thought of as a subset of post-traumatic stress disorder (PTSD), which is more commonly related to soldiers' postwar experiences. The symptoms of nightmares, persistent fear that the violence will recur, anxiety reactions, phobias, and emotional lability that battered women experience may be quite similar to the experiences of postwar veterans diagnosed with PTSD.

The reliance on PTSD as an explanatory framework for understanding and treating battered women is increasing among feminist professional therapists. Although there are dangers inherent in any diagnostic labeling (e.g., the person may become seen as the diagnosis), PTSD at least identifies external threats as precipitants and features an understanding of the disorder as a normal reaction to severe stress and trauma, albeit with unhealthy effects. Mary Ann Dutton (1992) discusses battered women's behavior within the PTSD framework, emphasizing that battered women are not sick but are in a sick situation. Her model for counseling reiterates the principles of feminist therapy and the recommendations of Walker: Ensure the battered woman's safety, empower her to choose, assist her in healing from psychological trauma. Similarly, Judith Herman (1992) places battered women in the larger category of patients who suffer from PTSD. Her historical overview of the symptoms and etiology associated with this disorder include the hysteria patients of Freud's day, the shell-shocked patients of World War II and the Vietnam war, political hostages and prisoners of war as well as victims of incest, rape, and battering. Herman, however, argues that a distinct diagnosis is needed for those who, like battered women, suffer long-term, chronic, repeated trauma. She suggests "complex PTSD." In any event, Herman's view of the stages of recovery for battered women and other PTSD patients is similar to that of Dutton and Walker: establishing safety, empowerment, and healing.

Others have also compared the battered women's situation to war survivors (Ochberg, 1988). PTSD and battered women's syndrome do not contradict the cycle theory of violence but extend it to consider psychological outcomes over the longer term of a relationship. Treatment focuses are similar to those detailed above (Walker, 1984b, 1994).

Graham, Rawlings, and Rimini (1988) liken the battered woman's situation to that of hostages. They focus on an interpretation of the reasons battered women retain their feelings of love for the abuser. They borrow the Stockholm syndrome, a model that accounts for the paradoxical feelings of care and concern expressed by hostages toward their captors. They propose that some battered women, like hostages, live in a state of terror for their lives. These women feel they cannot escape, so their very lives depend on the threatening person. Moreover, due to their isolation, the only available perspective on their situation is provided by the abuser, and the abuser is seen as the only possible source of kindness and concern. In such situations, battered women, like hostages, may come to identify with the aggressor through the psychological mechanism of traumatic bonding (Dutton & Painter, 1981). One of Graham et al.'s suggestions for treatment involves providing the battered woman with the constructs of the Stockholm model as a way of normalizing her experience. Dutton and Painter underscore the distress battered women will feel at the loss of relationship and urge therapists to prepare the woman for such an experience while allowing her to mourn that loss.

Gondolf (1988) proposes yet another model for considering the behavior of battered women and implications for treatment. In some respects, his model is a return to the grassroots emphasis on social system change over victim change. He criticizes Walker's learned helplessness hypothesis as leading to conceptualizations of battered women as helpless, passive victims. He offers an alternative conceptualization of battered women as survivors who increase their help-seeking behavior over time, rather than giving up and becoming psychologically paralyzed. Gondolf goes further in contending that it is the help sources, rather than the battered woman, that exhibit learned helplessness. The battered woman is coping and struggling, in a very logical and assertive fashion, to escape or end the abuse.

Still, Gondolf (1988) does not completely give up on psychological explanations of battered women's behavior. He suggests that the low self-esteem, guilt, self-blame, and depression that are often seen in battered women may represent a kind of temporary traumatic shock to the abuse, requiring "not so much psychotherapy as time and space to recuperate" (p. 21). A second possibility offered by Gondolf is that such symptoms may represent an effort on the part of the battered woman to save the relationship by acknowledging her alleged shortcomings and failure to be nurturing, supporting, or loving enough to make the marriage work. This, too, Gondolf proposes as a temporary sense of failure, quite different from the "sense of an uncontrollable universe which underlies learned helplessness" (p. 22). Finally, Gondolf suggests that symptoms of depression and guilt may represent an expression of separation anxiety that naturally accompanies leaving the abuser. He points not only to the economic realities that will make survival difficult but also to the realistic fears of reprisals and continued threat from the abuser. Gondolf concludes that it is our community systems of care and intervention—human services, police, courts, clergy—that need treatment. Moreover, he argues for an infusion of feminine values, based on nurturance and relatedness, into the patriarchal institutions of male dominance to transform that system.

Gondolf's reconceptualization of battered women's behavior and his development of a survivor hypothesis come directly out of his work with the Texas shelter movement and so reflect a grassroots feminist emphasis. Similarly, in an effort to define battered women's behaviors more positively, PCADV has developed the concept of a victim-survivor continuum for battered women. In the program model PCADV writes,

> A battered woman may be thought to fall along a victim-survivor continuum, depending on her own development and self-identification. All battered women have been victimized and in some sense all are survivors. But a woman may cease being a victim in her own eyes once she acknowledges her initial victimization and moves on to change her situation. She may then become a survivor, ready to help others move from victim to survivor. (PCADV, 1987, glossary [pages not numbered])

More recent theoretical developments have gone beyond the notions of battered women as either victims or survivors. In effect, writers such as Bonnie Burstow (1992), Ann Jones (1994), and Laura Brown (1994) have reinvoked the pro-woman line of the early radical feminists by presenting battered women as active resisters to their battering situation. These writers also come closest to identifying the social changes that need to be made to move toward a world in which woman battering no longer occurs. Burstow and Brown, in particular, ground their radical feminist therapy approaches in the need for social change.

This review of the feminist psychological theories dealing with battered women establishes that a variety of theoretical constructs exists, even among feminist therapists, for understanding the psychological state of battered women and their counseling needs. Although Walker's theories mostly emphasize the depressive psychological state that comes about after years of battering, she also acknowledges some of the material needs of individual battered women—needs for safety, occupational and other economic needs, and the need to end the relationship. Walker also recommends allowing the woman to gain power in the therapy relationship, though she stops short of recommending that the woman might also gain power through political activity. Gondolf provides an effective counter to Walker by defining the battered woman as a survivor, rather than a victim, and focusing on treating the helping systems (a political strategy). Brown and Burstow go even further by positing the battered woman as an active resister to her oppression in the relationship.

Feminist Activists; Feminist Therapists

Some of the differences we see in the approaches of Walker, Gondolf, Brown, and Burstow echo back to the tensions between the grassroots activists within the battered women's movement and professionally trained feminist therapists. As an activist in the movement who was also professionally trained as a psychologist, I wanted to bridge this tension-filled space between feminist activists and feminist therapists. I based the case study research that will be described in the following chapter on the assumption that there had to be a conceptual connection between the radical feminist analysis of women's oppression, the goals of social change, and the counseling efforts in battered women's programs. As it turned out, the counselors in my case study appeared to simultaneously hold parts of both the grassroots and the professional feminist analyses. But there was little indication that these counselors had achieved the kind of integrated conceptual bridge I had envisioned, for they seemed to haphazardly implement one or the other conception in their work at various times. In working with battered women, the counselors also employed many of the interventions suggested in the professional feminist literature (e.g. crisis intervention, groups, shelter, a grief model) as therapeutic or helping techniques. Yet, the women who work in these programs tend to discount all theoretical influences on women-helping-women, or counseling, by denigrating both theory and therapy as professionalism (Whalen, 1988). Thus, the theories or models of counseling they held, and from which, I contend, they inevitably operated, were typically not articulated. My research was an effort to articulate and explicate those internal frameworks and to describe the counselors' understandings of the feminist ideology within the battered women's movement and its influence on their counseling model.

Ellyn Kaschak's Framework

Ellyn Kaschak's work (1981) was influential in my early conceptualizing about my research. She offers some interesting distinctions among various feminist approaches to counseling. She considers a total of 22 aspects of therapy and compares them across five categories of therapy, including radical grassroots feminist, radical professional feminist, liberal professional feminist, nonsexist, and traditional psychoanalytic. Because battered women's programs began as grassroots radical feminist efforts, it occurred to me that a radical grassroots feminist therapy might offer not only a viable model for comparison to the model developed from the participants' responses in my case study but also a framework from which to develop a more clearly articulated subversive counseling model.

Kaschak (1981) first offers some striking distinctions between feminist and traditional therapies. For example, although feminist therapists acknowledge the value-laden and political aspects of therapy, traditional therapists purport a value-neutral, apolitical therapy. Although feminist therapists view psychopathology as the result of oppression, traditional therapists rely on intrapsychic constructs to explain psychopathology. And although feminist therapists work to challenge traditional sex roles and promote other societal changes, traditional therapists reinforce traditional sex roles and promote adjustment to societal norms.

Kaschak (1981) also considers specific differences between liberal feminist and radical feminist therapies. For example, radical feminist therapists seek to change society at its core, but liberal feminist therapists advocate amending existing societal institutions to promote equal opportunity between men and women. Furthermore, radical feminist therapists seek to abolish traditional sex roles, whereas liberal feminist therapists support women choosing sex-specific roles if they wish. Moreover, radical feminist therapists work to decrease the power differences between therapist and client, but liberal feminist therapists use that differential to empower the client.

But I was primarily drawn to the distinctions Kaschak (1981) makes between radical grassroots feminist therapists and radical professional feminist therapists. Although more subtle than the distinctions described above, they have particular relevance both for considering some of the responses of counselors in my case study and for developing the components of a subversive counseling model. After all, the battered women's movement considers itself a radical grassroots feminist movement and it promotes the notion of professionals as Other—even professional feminist counselors, radical or not. In its effort to exorcise professionalist approaches to working with battered women, the movement has dichotomized the subtle distinctions that Kaschak has enumerated.

Kaschak's research indicates that for the issues of feminist analysis, political application of feminism in therapy, therapist values, proposed sex-role changes, expressions of women's sexuality, use of anger, rejection of transference, and the importance of gender of therapist, there are no essential differences between radical grassroots and radical professional feminist therapists. The understandings about the sources of pathology, the goals of therapy, and the client-counselor relationship, however, were the factors she found that most clearly differentiated radical grassroots from radical professional feminist therapists.

Radical grassroots feminist therapists view all pathology as socially determined. This conviction is shared with the antipsychiatrists (cf. Szasz, 1970) and radical therapists (Agel, 1971) and is an echo from the pro-woman line of radical feminists: Women are not sick; society is sick. Thus, society ought to be the focus of change rather than the individual. By contrast, radical professional feminist therapists view psychopathology as both societally rooted and the result of individual development. This conviction begins to shift the focus for solutions from the societal systems to the individual.

For the goals of therapy, radical grassroots feminist therapists theoretically hold that clients must participate in social change activities, for only these kinds of activities work on the source of the problem in society. Radical professional feminist therapists, on the other hand, believe that client participation in social change is preferable but not mandatory. Such therapists hold that political activity is not for everyone and that individual clients may have other, more immediate needs. Although they acknowledge that a part of their professional obligation is to work for social change, they do not think it essential for the battered women client to engage in such work.

For the client-therapist relationship, radical grassroots feminist therapists assert that any difference in power is inappropriate, but radical professional feminist therapists acknowledge the inherent power differential in the relationship and use their power to share and develop personal power in the client (cf. Douglas, 1985). Radical grassroots feminist therapists hold that the therapist is not an expert, but radical professional feminist therapists argue that the therapist has certain skills and expertise that she shares with the client (cf. Lerman, 1985). Radical grassroots feminists believe that contact with clients outside the therapy sessions is both appropriate and desirable, as both clients and therapists are part of a women's community. Radical professional feminist therapists tend to limit outside client contact to some social or political situations.

Kaschak's framework for understanding the differences among various kinds of feminist approaches to therapy was useful to me as I considered the kind of counseling model I expected to find in battered women's programs. I expected to find that the activists I interviewed would make no references to the psychological effects of individual development; that social change activities would be an integral part of the counseling-helping effort; and that the counselors I interviewed would be, in every sense, peers to the battered women who come for help. These counselors would view themselves as having no particular expertise, skills, or knowledge. They would believe in the value of friendships with battered women who come to shelter, perhaps continuing that friendship in other contexts after the battered woman no longer needs the help of shelter or the program. I expected to find that in the battered women's movement, as among all radical feminist therapists, counselors explicitly include a feminist analysis in their work with battered women and use that analysis to educate about the ways women as a group are oppressed and about the need for social change. Moreover, battered women's counselors would state their own value bases and not pretend to be neutral helpers. They would offer suggestions to help expand sex-role options, would promote woman-defined expressions of sexuality, and would validate the client's anger as a motivator for change. In addition, they would deny and ignore any suggestion that the battered woman is transferring her feelings for another onto them. Rather, they would take what the woman says at face value, refusing to interpret additional meanings. Finally, they would agree with the notion that women are best suited to helping women and, in particular, battered women are best suited to helping battered women.

It turned out that these distinctions were indeed useful in analyzing the response of counselors in my case study, but I did not find a consistent identification with either category of therapists. The participants sometimes offered conceptualizations that fit the radical grassroots feminist therapy model, but at other times their ideas fit the radical professional feminist therapy model. They also offered concepts from humanism, from behaviorism and social learning theory, and even from object relations theory. Overall, they failed to avoid the fatal trap of individual psychological understandings and its implication for identifying the locus of the problem of woman battering.

Case Study

Counseling in Feminist Social Change Programs

In 1991, I completed a case study on counseling in Pennsylvania battered women and anti-rape programs. This study led to the development of descriptive models of counseling, of the ideology of the movements, and of the influence of ideology on counseling. Although the counselors were not always internally coherent or consistent in their approach to their work, the research process and the model-building activity helped me formulate the categories of thought that needed to be represented in a radical feminist counseling model that was aimed at political subversion. More important, the research helped clarify my expectations and refine my understandings of the disjuncture between our models for social change and our models for counseling. In short, this case study established that there was a need for a social change model and a counseling model that were congruent with one another.

Methodological Considerations

To answer my basic research questions—what counseling model was conceived by counselors working in feminist social change programs, and how did the ideology of the social movement inform that model—it was necessary to employ a qualitative research approach. Naturalistic inquiry (Lincoln & Guba, 1985) provided the overarching framework for the development of the specific method used for this study. But I also relied on readings about feminist research approaches (Stanley & Wise, 1983) and I was committed to the development of grounded theory (Glaser & Straus, 1967) that would have real meaning and effects for movement workers and for victims of male violence.

As a psychologist trained in experimental design, I was initially concerned about questions of statistical significance, random selection, and sample size, and how these might affect the reliability, generalizability, and validity of my findings. These issues, however, become framed somewhat differently when one is employing qualitative research methods. Naturalistic inquiry, a method derived from sociological field studies, seeks to generate theory that is grounded in the real-life contexts of people's lives. In contrast to experimental approaches, naturalistic inquiry does not seek to isolate variables, to test theory, or to statistically generalize its specific findings to larger populations. Rather, it seeks to develop conceptual categories, or themes, and theoretical models that can later be considered and further developed through research with contrasting populations or in contrasting contexts. Naturalistic inquiry relies on the idiographic interpretations of the researcher, who uses his or her subjective stance with relation to the study to further his or her understanding of the data. In other words, different researchers, studying the same data, are likely to interpret the data differently and develop different conceptual schemes to help explain and clarify the themes that emerge.

Thus, for this case study, it was not my intent, nor is it possible by using this research approach, to generalize the findings to the larger population of counselors (or even counselors working in feminist social movement programs). My goal was to build a conceptual model from the data of the interviews, a model that would help organize and explain the relationships among the ideas these counselors held about their work. This model might then provide battered women's counselors an opportunity both to review the relationship between their ideology and their practice and to assess the coherence of that relationship. In addition, the model could now be considered in relation to the conceptualizations of other counselors in other contexts. As it is so considered, it can be refined, filled out, and amended for those contexts. And so the theory will continue to be built.

Specifically, this research was designed as a case study of counselors working in domestic violence and sexual assault programs in Pennsylvania. I interviewed a total of eight counselors from programs in different geographical regions of Pennsylvania. From these interviews, I derived a descriptive model of the conceptualizations held by counselors about their counseling work with women victims of male violence. I also derived a descriptive model of their conceptualizations about the ideology of the social movements in which they worked. These models were based on my grouping of themes that seemed to be related, rather than an attempt to represent the approach used by any one of the counselors. In fact, the counselors did not consistently work from any particular model. Finally, I considered the influence of the counselors' understandings of ideology on their counseling work.

The method of naturalistic inquiry features a conceptual interaction between the data and the researcher's experience, ideas, and theories. In this case, as researcher I brought my experience within the battered women's movement, my ideas about the need for social change, and my theoretical understandings of feminism and counseling to bear on the data, that is, the verbalizations of participants about their counseling work in feminist social change programs. The semistructured interview I developed was designed to elicit discourse from the counselors about how they thought about their counseling work, the ideology of the social movement in which they were working, and the influence of that ideology on their counseling practice. For counseling, I wanted to know what clients say to counselors when they first sit down together, how they describe why they are there, how they talk about what they want, need, hope for, expect as a result of meeting with the counselor. I kept my questions open-ended to allow participants to take off in the direction that made sense to them, to produce a quantity of verbalization about these domains, and to allow them to think out loud, so that I could better analyze their conceptualizing process.

Although themes or categories of conceptualizations may be said to *emerge* from the data, the organization of those themes and the filling in or framing of less fully developed (less data-saturated) categories come largely from the researcher. So although it was partly my obligation to faithfully describe the participant's ideas, it was also my task to build a coherent theoretical model from that description.

I was initially concerned that my questions might provide a frame for the conceptual categories that I hoped would emerge from the data. In reflecting on the work I did in 1991, I would accept that argument when it comes to the social movement model I developed. In response to the open-ended questions I asked, these counselors said very little about the social movement. I had to ask more specific questions about the movement, and therefore, my questions clearly framed the conceptual categories derived to analyze the counselors' ideas in this realm. But I do not believe that this criticism is valid for the counseling model I will describe. Instead, those categories emerged from and depend on the particular ideas about counseling that have salience for the participants.

In my research proposal for this project, I reviewed metaconstructs of counseling theories and discussed five features of most counseling models: client-counselor relationship, theory of the nature of symptoms, process of counseling, techniques used, and goals of counseling. My initial interview contained several questions designed to elicit discourse about these aspects of counseling; however, the participants in this study did not organize their thinking about counseling in quite this way. Rather, they spoke about what they do in counseling, yielding a conceptual category I called Counseling Interventions, which includes parts of process, techniques, and goals. Participants also spoke of what women seek and need from counseling, yielding a conceptual category I called Women's Needs, which also includes ideas about the goals and techniques of counseling. Moreover, rather than speaking about the nature of symptoms, participants typically spoke of the kinds of problems women came to them with, yielding a conceptual category I called Women's Problems. However, the feature Counselor-Client Relationship did have salience and importance for these counselors, and their discourse about this topic yielded a conceptual category by that name.

My point in illustrating this process of analysis is to establish the legitimacy of the assertion that the conceptual categories I describe for the counseling model did emerge from the data of the interview, rather than being imposed by my questions. The fact that I was disappointed in the models that emerged from my interviews with these counselors, coupled with the fact that the data did not fit my preconceived notions of what I would find, says something positive about the validity and integrity of naturalistic inquiry as a method. It was this sense of disappointment that eventually led to the writing of this book and the elaboration of a counseling model that I believe better fits the ideology of radical feminism and the battered women's movement.

The Counseling Model

Although my original research involved both domestic violence and sexual assault counselors, I will focus here on the understandings and interventions of these counselors in their work with battered women. The counseling model, derived from the original research, consisted of five counseling submodels, or approaches, of theoretically related subcategories. Table 6.1 depicts the categories, the counseling approaches, and the theoretical relationships among subcategories within the approaches.

The primary conceptual categories derived from the interviews are listed in the left-hand column of the table: Women's Problems, Women's Needs, Counseling Interventions, Counselor Role, and Counselor-Client Relationship. Looking *across* the table, there are five subcategories within each primary category; that is, five different ways of conceiving, for example, Women's Problems or Women's Needs when a battered woman comes to the program for help. The subcategories are theoretically related to each other *down* each of the columns, forming five approaches of counseling that I have termed the Resource, Educational, Psychological, Medical, and Political approaches. Despite this theoretical relationship, the subcategories and the counseling approaches are not mutually exclusive or constructed with rigid boundaries. There is conceptual overlap, with some concepts shading into two or more subcategories. It is important to remember that these subcategories are arranged in an order that I believe makes theoretical sense. All of the primary categories and their subcategories emerged from my interviews, but the counselors did not necessarily discuss them in the organized way I am presenting them here. In fact, each of the counselors in the case study moved in and out of these conceptual categories, and no one strictly adhered to one theoretical submodel. Also, some of the subcategories and counseling approaches were used much more frequently than others by the counselors. I will return to this point later.

TABLE 6.1 The Counseling Model

Counseling Approaches

Conceptual Category	Resource	Educational	Psychological	Medical	Political
Women's Problems	Basic Survival	False Beliefs	Self-Doubts	Illness	Sociopolitical
Women's Needs	Survival Tools	Alternative Education	Relational Experiences	Symptom Treatment	Social Change
Counseling Interventions	Directive	Confrontive-Didactic	Supportive-Empowerment	Therapeutic	Social Action
Counselor Role	Consultant	Educator	Companion	Therapist	Social Activist
Counselor-Client Relationship	Consultant-Seeker	Teacher-Student	Woman-to-Woman	Doctor-Patient	Member-Initiate

It is a difficult task to describe the process of analyzing 30 or more hours of interviews. I found it remarkably similar to the process of analyzing the discourse of clients in counseling. It is a process that requires both time and some ability to let go of one's preconceptions so that the conceptual world of the client can be heard and understood. The process in research like this, however, is multiplied, because the conceptualizations of eight different people were being pooled, compared, contrasted, and analyzed.

As I worked to analyze the first interviews, I tentatively formed some conceptual categories that I identified as central issues for the counselors. That is to say, the first two or three counselors I interviewed seemed to have a great deal to say about the topics of women's problems and women's needs. These two categories served as primary classifications, out of which I then subcategorized the variety of ideas about women's problems and needs. As I worked with these subcategories further, I began to see connections between the subcategories across conceptual categories. For example, when women's problems were defined as physical abuse, their needs were for escape or safety. Subsequent interviews filled out these categories and also raised additional domains of emphasis that eventually coalesced into new conceptual categories. Those categories were further subcategorized until I was able to discern a pattern of relationships among these subcategories across all the primary categories.

A thorough explication of each of the five primary categories (Women's Problems, Women's Needs, Counseling Interventions, Counselor Role, and Counselor-Client Relationship) and their subcategories is provided in my dissertation. For my purposes here, a summary will suffice. Overall, the analysis I developed suggested that the ways in which women's problems were defined in turn determined women's counseling needs, which helped determine the counseling intervention style. The intervention style then helped determine the counselor role, which in turn determined the structure and function of the counselor-client relationship.

Primary Conceptual Categories

Women's Problems. Women's problems were conceptualized in the following ways. Most frequently, problems were viewed as Basic Survival issues. That is, women initially defined their problems when they sought help from a domestic violence program in terms of the abuse they were experiencing in their current lives. As counselors elaborated on their initial responses, descriptions emerged that suggested part of the problem counselors dealt with was ignorance or False Beliefs of women, based on not only the way women in general are socialized but also the particular socialization experiences of some women. Many responses identified problems as centered around women's Self-Doubts. Some of these responses were similar to those in the False Beliefs subcategory, in that counselors suggested that women think and believe something the counselors in these interviews implied is not true. The primary difference in the two subcategories, as I defined them, was in the problem source. The former, False Beliefs, was based on early learning and socialization experiences and might be rectified by new information and learning. Self-Doubts, on the other hand, came about as a result of abuse itself, that is, living a life controlled by someone else. The subcategory Self-Doubts implied a more pervasive problem and a more sustained counseling intervention. Self-Doubts was really a shorthand term for problems in motivation, a lack of belief in self-efficacy, and pervasive self-deprecation. The subcategory was similar in many respects to Walker's concept of learned helplessness in battered women. A few responses suggested Illness and symptom concepts about the problems presented to counselors. Illness concepts included not only mental illness diagnoses but physical illness and psychological illness labels, such as low self-esteem, dependency, or hypervigilance. Less than half of the counselors I interviewed offered problem statements that clearly came out of a feminist Sociopolitical analysis that spoke to the pathology of society, rather than the pathology of the individual. Counselors, when they did respond from this framework, equated symptoms, which a more traditional approach would label as pathological, with behaviors a woman employs to stay as safe as she is able to in a world characterized by others exerting power over her. They analyzed that it is women's lot in society to deal with the exertion of power and control, but they normalized women's responses: "What appear to be symptoms" are behaviors women use to help them be safe, to avoid battering. This analysis is conceptually tied to the pro-woman line of some of the early radical feminists.

Women's Needs. Women's needs were defined primarily by the ways in which the counselor thought about the presenting problems. Most women were seen as needing Survival Tools or material resources to survive and avoid further abuse. Many of the counselors thought that women needed an Alternative Education to relearn much of what they were taught growing up in our society as women. Counselors also thought, however, that women needed Relational Experiences with other women who had also experienced abuse—a relational relearning, as distinct from informa- tion-based learning. Some counselors spoke of the need for Symptom Treatment, implying a physical or psychological problem that needed remediation or healing. For example, battered women were sometimes viewed as needing treatment for depression or treatment to build self- esteem. Counselors framed only a few of their responses to the probes about what women need in terms of Social Change. These few responses reflected both radical and liberal feminist political analyses of the problems in society. Some counselors, echoing the ideology of radical feminists, thought that women's problems are created by "the patriarchy," and so the patriarchy must be overturned. More often, however, counselors were quite tentative in their assessment of the need for clients to be involved in political action and instead focused on their own support of liberal feminism's efforts both to change laws harmful to women and to enforce existing laws that protect women.

Counseling Interventions. Counseling interventions varied according to the ways in which Women's Problems and Needs were defined. Direc- tive interventions were used to assist women in getting their legal rights and material needs met. Confrontive-Didactic interventions aided the process of reeducating the woman to a different (i.e., feminist) understanding of women, women's roles, and women's relationships to men. Supportive- Empowering interventions were mentioned almost as frequently as the confrontive style. These interventions were viewed as helping a woman become more comfortable with herself and helping her develop more self-respect and a sense of personal power. Some counselors used the word *spirituality* to refer to this self-developmental work, but most described the intervention in terms of empowerment. A few responses could be classified as Therapeutic interventions, that is, directed toward specific symptom alleviation or illness cure. The illnesses specified included multiple personality disorder, depression, codependency, alcohol or drug abuse, and low self-esteem. Social Action intervention responses were given infrequently when study participants were talking about their counseling. But just as some counselors had identified women's problems as social pathology and women's needs as sociopolitical change, there were a few suggestions for counseling interventions based on social action on the part of the counselor, though rarely on the part of the client.

Counselor Role. Definitions of the counselor role arose out of the previous analysis. When counselors assumed a directive intervention style, they viewed their role as that of a Consultant. In serving as consultant, the counselor worked with the client to inform her of resources, to clarify the available options, and to advocate on her behalf so that she might more readily implement her decisions. When counselors initiated confrontive and didactic interventions, their role was that of an Educator. Companion seemed to best describe the role of a counselor who was acting to support and empower the client. The subcategory Therapist is logically deducible from problems defined as illness, needs for symptom alleviation, and therapeutic interventions. The closest any of the participants came, however, to identifying the counselor role as that of therapist was when they spoke of themselves as helping people heal from their pain. Most of the counselors rejected outright the term *therapist.* On the whole, these counselors were more comfortable with the notion of themselves as Social Activists than they were with social action as a counseling intervention. Several of them spoke of their role as advocates with community institutions and agencies. A few talked about social action as legislative work— writing legislators to support new laws or new programs. Others talked about ongoing educative work with the local police, to better ensure fair and adequate treatment of victims. One mentioned demonstrations like Take Back the Night marches and speak-outs. She saw it as her role to participate in and sometimes organize such activities.

Counselor-Client Relationship. The counselor-client relationship was defined out of the conceptualization of the role of the counselor. For my dissertation, I decided it was important to separately examine hierarchy and power in the relationship between counselor and client, because this feature of relationships has particular salience for the counselors interviewed and also for feminist theorists. All of the counselors I interviewed maintained that the relationship between the counselor and the client should be egalitarian and nonhierarchical (as do many feminist therapists). Each further maintained that her way of relating to clients was egalitarian and nonhierarchical. Indeed, if there were any hierarchy, it was the client who was viewed as holding the more powerful position, for she controlled the counseling; however, the counselors' descriptions of the roles of counselors did not always conform to this nonhierarchical notion of how the relationship ought to be structured. For purposes of this summary, I will forego the analysis of power within each of the relationships outlined below, except to say that each inevitably contains elements of hierarchy and power discrepancies between counselor and client. My view of the role of power and hierarchy in my proposed counseling model will be discussed in the following chapter.

The relationship of Consultant-Seeker arose out of the conceptual notion that the counselor's role is that of consultant. A consultant is someone engaged by a person who is seeking help because it is assumed the consultant has some knowledge or ability not readily available to the consultee or client. In the business world, the proper analogy might be consultant-client, for a consultant is hired by a client. In this context of battered women's programs, no fees are charged for counseling, so the more appropriate term for the person who is obtaining consultation is *seeker.* The relationship of Teacher-Student arose from notions of the counselor's role as that of educator when the counselors viewed themselves as "pouring knowledge into" the client; for example, when they informed clients of their legal rights in a relationship or when they taught expanded notions of women's roles. The Woman-to-Woman relationship was affirmed most often by the counselors I interviewed, particularly when they saw themselves as companions to the battered women who came to them for help. Within this relationship, counselors saw themselves as leading women to question their experiences, assumptions, and prior learning. What was being taught, through this relationship, was not a set of facts, as in the consulting or teacher-student relationship. Rather, a set of beliefs—the client's worldview—was being gently challenged while a new set of beliefs —the counselor's—was being offered. Counselors viewed this as a nonhierarchical, egalitarian relationship that allowed the battered woman to experience herself in a new way. I also included a subcategory of Doctor-Patient because it is the logical extension of the counselor role seen as that of therapist, yet none of the counselors I interviewed described the counselor-client relationship in this way. Several, in fact, denounced this style of relationship because it is the style of traditional mental health treatment (of which they largely disapprove) and because of their affirmation that women are not sick. But it was the relationship of Member-Initiate that I was most interested in. I theorized that this style of relationship might well emanate from the counselor's role as social activist. It seemed to me that to the extent that battered women did take part in political action for social change, whether by talking at speak-outs, marching in demonstrations, writing their legislators, or becoming volunteers in the program, these women were initiate members in the social movement represented by the program. The counselors in this research, however, even though they might formerly have been active participants in the early women's liberation movement, rarely acknowledged this recruitment aspect of their work. Even one counselor, who saw herself as a radical feminist of the 1960s and "really thought we were going to change the world," now says she never tries to impose her feminist philosophy on clients:

> "That's my belief, not necessarily theirs. If you really believe in empowerment, to be an effective counselor, you must be willing to give up that control and really believe that's what's best for the client. She must come to her own realizations, even if it's anti-feminist." (quoted in Whalen, 1992, p. 231)

As I will elaborate in the following chapter, it seems to me that part of the role of social activist is to promote a vision of a better world and encourage others to join in the struggle to achieve that vision. One of the important potential effects of the counseling effort in battered women's programs is that a vision of a nonviolent world becomes shared by increasing numbers of women. Moreover, the hope is that increasing numbers of women will join and become consciously a part of the social movement that is working toward that vision. The nature of the member-initiate relationship is such that as soon as the initiate joins the group, she is a member, and all the feelings of "communitas" associated with being a member of the group are available to her. Thus, engaging in social change activities not only benefits the movement but also is healing for the individual. It was apparent from my interviews, however, that few of the counselors shared my enthusiasm for this being an important role for counselors within the battered women's movement.

Counseling Approaches

Five counseling approaches emerged through this research. Each approach contained differing conceptualizations of women's problems, women's needs, counseling interventions, counselor role, and counselor-client relationship. The labels I developed for each of the submodels capture the essence of each approach. As displayed in Table 6.1, the submodels are labeled the Resource, Educational, Psychological, Medical, and Political approaches to counseling.

Resource Approach. Within the Resource approach, women's problems are understood by counselors as problems of survival, so women's needs from counseling were for survival tools. Battered women, when initially seeking help from a domestic violence program, begin by describing their experiences of abuse within their intimate relationship. Even when they question whether these experiences ought to be labeled abusive or violent, the problems they talk about are reflective of their partner's exercise of power and control and are labeled abuse, violence, and threat by the counselor. The battered woman's immediate problem is how to survive this abuse, and her need is for survival tools, such as escape plans, shelter or safe housing, information about resources, and legal protection. Counseling interventions tend to be directive, because the counselor is letting the woman know what resources are available and how she might best access those resources. The counselor might be likely to tell the woman directly that she needs to come to the shelter to be safe or she needs to get a protection order through the legal system. The counselor role is that of consultant, whereas the client role is that of seeker. The battered woman needs information and resources to get safe, and the counselor can help her access those tools.

Educational Approach. Within the Educational approach, women's problems are understood as false beliefs that women acquire through the traditional sex-role socialization process in our culture. Their counseling need, therefore, is for an alternative education about women and sex roles. Battered women often talk about how they view their role within the intimate relationship as the woman, the wife or lover, the nurturer, the supporter. They frequently view themselves as the cause of the violence they experience and thus seek to improve their performance of these social roles. Consequently they suppress any desires or thoughts they might have about alternative behaviors or roles that don't fit these definitions. For example, they might not consider going back to college, working outside the home, or following their own interests. The counselors in my study sometimes viewed the battered woman as overly socialized into her role as woman. In these situations, the counselor assumes a didactic and confrontive intervention style, attempting to teach the battered woman about her rights as a human being and challenging her to consider other roles and modes of behavior. The counselor's role becomes that of a teacher, and the client is her student.

Psychological Approach. The Psychological approach is an extension of the educational approach in that the psychological approach also entails learning. When women's problems are thought of as arising out of self-doubts, women's counseling needs are viewed as relational relearning that might come about through the counseling experience with another woman who has also been victimized by male violence. Battered women were often viewed by these counselors as psychologically injured by their experiences of abuse and violence. As a result of this injury, battered women may be filled with doubts about their identity and integrity as a person. The counselor, usually another battered woman, is thought of as a companion to a client in her learning process. The counselor builds a relationship with the battered woman by supporting and validating her experiences as a woman and empowers the woman to redefine and take control of her life. Together, counselor and client engage in an ongoing process of consciousness-raising about women.

Medical Approach. The Medical approach was much less frequently invoked by these counselors. At times, some symptoms seemed to have been viewed as signs of illness that could be alleviated through treating the symptom. For example, battered women were sometimes labeled as depressed or suffering from low self-esteem, as if alleviating these symptoms would be a primary goal of counseling. These counselors, however, tended to use intervention styles and assume roles described in the other approaches, rather than assuming the role of therapist or doctor. The conception of the client as patient was strongly rejected.

Political Approach. The Political approach, as a unit, was invoked somewhat more frequently than the medical approach, but less often than the first three approaches discussed above. Women's problems were often understood in sociopolitical terms; that is, battered women were often viewed as victims who exemplified the oppression of women in patriarchal society. Most counselors believed that social change for women was sorely needed, but social action was rarely suggested as a counseling intervention for the client. Clearly, many of these counselors saw themselves as social activists; however, they did not actively recruit their clients to join the social movement in which they worked.

For my dissertation report, I weighted the responses of counselors within each of the subcategories, and overall for each of the counseling approaches, to analyze which subcategories and approaches were more frequently used. The preferred, most frequently emphasized and employed conceptual strategies were located within the Psychological approach. Next in the counselors' preference were the Resource and Educational approaches. These two approaches were employed with similar emphasis (to each other) and almost as frequently as the Psychological approach. Much less frequently relied on was the Political approach. Although that approach was still popular as a means of analyzing women's needs and the role of counselor, counselors did not often advocate social action as part of their counseling interventions, nor did they attempt to recruit clients into social action groups. The Medical approach was rarely invoked, and were it not for occasional references by the counselors to specific symptoms (as discussed above), it would not be a part of the overall model.

The Social Movement Model

Recall that my research was originally based on the idea that the feminist social change ideology of the battered women's movement would result in a counseling approach that included social change strategies and goals. I first tried to assess the counseling models held by counselors who worked in feminist social change programs by focusing my questions on how they thought about their helping efforts and what they did in counseling sessions with women. I did not want to contaminate these responses with a prior discussion about the broader social movement and its ideology. But once the counselors had thoroughly discussed their ideas about

counseling, I turned the interview to a discussion of these broader ideological issues. To describe the counselors' conceptualizations of the social
movement in which they worked, I developed several probes to elicit
discourse about the counselors' understanding of the ideology of the
movement; however, I was unable to obtain many elaborated concepts.
The relative paucity of responses about the social movement was in
contrast to my expectations. The philosophy and ideology of the anti-rape
and battered women's movements had always been important to me both
in understanding my own counseling work and in overseeing the program
and staff of which I was director. Moreover, many of my discussions with
other directors across the state and my work on various coalition commit-
tees had included ideological issues. Consequently, I was surprised that
these counselors seemed to struggle conceptually with their responses
to my questions about the social movement. As a result, the model I
developed to describe counselors' conceptualizations about the social
movement in which they worked is less data-saturated than the counseling
model, but it does offers an initial frame for understanding the counselors'
ideas about the philosophical bases of their work.

The social movement model that was developed from the interviews
with participants is comprised of three submodels, or sets of ideological
understandings, each containing differing conceptualizations of the social
problem definition, movement goals, means to achieve goals, and underlying philosophy. In contrast to those developed for the counseling model,
these conceptual categories—problem, goals, means, and philosophy—
did not emerge from the interview material in the same way as the
conceptual categories for the counseling model. Instead, the social movement categories are clearly framed and constituted by the particular
questions I asked. Had I been able to elicit more discussion from the
counselors about the social movement, different conceptual categories
might have emerged. Still, the subcategories of the primary conceptual
categories are closely tied to the interview data, and the resulting submodels do reflect, I believe, differing ideological perspectives on the
social movement in which these counselors work.

Following the organization of the previous discussion, I refer the reader
to Table 6.2, which depicts the resulting social movement model, its four
primary conceptual categories, and its three submodels or ideological sets.
As with the counseling model, the subcategories are theoretically related
to one another down each of the columns, forming three sets of social

TABLE 6.2 The Social Movement

	Movement Ideological Sets		
Conceptual Category	*Women's Affiliation Movement*	*Women's Equality Movement*	*Human Rights Movement*
Problem Definition	Women Not Valued	Power and Privilege	Social Learning
Movement Goal	Survival	Equal Power	Less Cultural Violence
Means to Achieve Goal	Building Women's Community	Social and Political Change	Individual Solutions
Movement Philosophy	Cultural Feminism	Liberal Feminism	Humanism

movement ideologies, which I will summarize after elucidating the primary conceptual categories.

Primary Conceptual Categories

Although all of the counselors I interviewed considered themselves to be a part of a social movement, each had somewhat different ideas about not only the philosophy and goals of the movement but also the means necessary to achieve those goals. I initially asked the counselors if they thought of either themselves or the program in which they were employed as being involved in a social movement. All agreed that they were a part of a social movement. Most of them responded with a simple yes to this question, acknowledging a sense of social movement involvement for themselves and for their program. Some made distinctions between their program's level of involvement in movement activities and their own.

Movement Name. Having assessed that all participants in the study thought of themselves as part of a social movement, I proceeded to ask them what they would call that movement. I was surprised to discover that the counselors had to struggle to come up with a phrase or term to name the movement. I had posed this question to get a sense of whether these counselors saw themselves as part of a larger women's movement or specifically involved in a movement around the focus of their program, for example, domestic violence. I was also interested in the language they might use to name the movement. For example, would they call it a "domestic violence movement" or a "battered women's movement"? These distinctions, it turned out, were not salient concerns for the counselors I interviewed.

The counselors' names for the social movement fell into three subcategories, which I used to constitute the basis for three submodels of social movement ideology. One set of ideological conceptualizations, which I called the Women's Affiliation ideology, was composed of ideas of the movement as a women's movement, with no particular goal identified. Another, the Women's Equality ideology, was conceptualized as a woman-focused movement for specific goals—for example, the liberation and empowerment of women and other oppressed groups. The third, which I referred to as a Human Rights ideology, did not include a gendered analysis but argued in favor of human (and victim) rights.

Social Problem Definition. Although the counselors had difficulty naming the movement, I thought they might be able to elaborate on the social problems the movement was seeking to address. This question was posed through a series of related probes about how counselors viewed the problem of domestic violence and what factors they thought created and maintained the problem. Many of the counselors' responses seemed to indicate that the problem of woman battering is based in the fact that Women [are] Not Valued in our society. That is, the problem of domestic violence was defined as based in a general cultural misogyny and devaluation of women.

There were also a number of responses that defined the problem in terms of Power and Privilege. These responses often contained specific references to sexism, patriarchy, or both and they identified the problem in gendered terms, by indicating women's lack of power and privilege relative to men. A number of counselors, responding from the framework of power and privilege, expanded their analyses beyond gender to consider other social structural inequalities based in such constructs as race or sexual orientation. Both sets of responses—those specific to a gendered analysis and those that include other groups—emphasize ideas about rights, power, and prejudicial attitudes resulting in discrimination and oppression for one group, power and privilege for the dominant group.

A third group of responses relied on individual explanations of violence as created by the effects of Social Learning. These responses pointed to the general cultural acceptance of and desensitization to violence. They argued that violence was learned in families and that there were few countervailing cultural messages to promote nonviolence. Moreover, these responses were not grounded in a gendered analysis of the problem. Instead, they employed gender-neutral terms such as *victim, perpetrator,* and *family.* From this perspective, perpetrators might be male or female; men and women both can learn domestic violence; and violence is learned in families and handed down intergenerationally. In emphasizing gender-neutrality and social learning, the conceptualizations tended to ignore problems specific to women as a group. The resulting analysis tended to (a) target abusers as needing help or remediation, (b) focus on victims' rights rather than women's rights, and (c) discuss the cultural acceptance of violence generally.

Movement Goals. I next asked the counselors, based on their notions of the social problem, about their ideas of the goals of the social movement in which they were involved. Some of the counselors identified the goal of the movement simply as Survival of the movement—to keep women affiliating together. Other responses had to do with establishing Equal Power among men and women. Again, within this framework, some counselors went beyond a focus on women gaining equal power to include an emphasis on equality for all groups. In transcending the category of gender, these counselors frequently advocated the elimination of all human differences, or at least the *perception* of human difference. The idea seemed to be that if the perception of differences were eliminated, there would be no prejudice, no discrimination, and no violence based in hatred of a particular group. A third set of responses framed the goal in terms of Less Cultural Violence. These counselors thought we needed to reduce the incidence of family violence and media displays of cultural violence to reduce the opportunities for exposure to violence that result in individuals learning to be violent. Some counselors, operating from this perspective, framed the goal of the movement as advancing and protecting the rights of victims. These ideas were offered in gender-neutral terms.

Means to Achieve Goals. I next asked the counselors how they thought we would achieve the goals they had defined. Or, how might we achieve a violence-free world? Some counselors thought that the way to achieve a violence-free world was through Building Women's Community. They wanted to promote women's affiliation with women and hoped to build a culture based in women's values.

A second cluster of responses focused on using Social and Political Change strategies to create an equal power structure for men and women. For those who went beyond gender to talk of other oppressed groups, education was viewed as key in eliminating the perception of difference and prejudice—not only sexism, but racism, homophobia, ageism, and all other "isms" based on difference. In particular, education, counseling, and remediation were often advocated for men. The idea seemed to be that if men, as the more powerful and privileged group, could be educated in a way to eliminate their prejudices, then equality for everyone would follow. Counselors who wanted to include men in this work believed they were treating only half the problem by working exclusively with women. Ideas about oppressed groups originate in conceptions of unequal power based on socially constructed categories of human difference. It is for this reason that I included the counselors' conceptions about equality that were based in a gendered analysis with those based in a broader oppression analysis. It was interesting to me that when these counselors used gender as a construct to analyze the social problem, they often advocated specific political strategies and changes. By contrast, when they used other constructs of oppression—for example, race, sexual orientation—they seemed to prefer education and attitude change as the means to achieve equality among peoples. As a result, this subcategory of responses promotes not only political change in laws and power structures but also social change in sex role socialization and prejudicial attitudes. Although I think education can be considered a social change tactic, it does not directly challenge existing power structures. Moreover, the shift from direct political strategies to education represents, I believe, a shift toward individual rather than social structural solutions. This shift toward individual solutions becomes even more emphatic in the following subcategory.

A third set of responses suggested that the primary way to achieve a world in which violence is reduced, thus lessening one's exposure to violence, is through legislation to protect potential and actual victims of violence. In addition, some counselors emphasized the need to therapeutically treat men and other perpetrators of violence. In other words, these responses tended to seek Individual Solutions or microcosmic explanations, rather than social or macrocosmic solutions, for the problem of violence.

Movement Philosophy. Only a few of the counselors volunteered ideas about the philosophy of the social movement in which they saw themselves involved. Their responses can be organized into subcategories that characterize the underlying philosophy of each of the three ideologies of the social movement model. The designations I used for those philosophies—Cultural Feminism, Liberal Feminism, and Humanism—come from the feminist literature, rather than from the language of the participants in this study. Part of the reason for my decision to use those terms was that the counselors did not name a philosophy. Instead, they described some beliefs, some goals, and some action plans relating to the other categories described above. In addition, I thought it was important to consider the movement's philosophy, as understood by these counselors, in terms of its historical origins in feminist thought. As it turned out, I could not be faithful to the data I collected if I labeled one of the Movement Philosophy subcategories as radical feminism. I will consider, in the concluding part of this section, the ways in which humanism and cultural and liberal feminism so permeated the conceptualizations of the participants in this research that radical feminism was often difficult to recognize.

Movement Ideological Sets

As I summarized earlier, the responses of the participants to the range of questions about the ideology of the social movement in which they worked appeared to coalesce into three sets of ideologies, which the reader can reference by reading down Table 6.2.

Women's Affiliation. Within the Women's Affiliation ideological set, the social problem of violence against women was conceptualized as being based in false beliefs about women and prejudiced attitudes and practices toward women as a group; that is, the problem is that women are not valued in our culture. From this viewpoint, the sole goal of the social movement is survival of the movement and survival of women. The means to achieve this goal is for women to keep affiliating with and valuing one another. By doing so, women will begin building an alternative culture: a women's community, based in women's values, that challenges and undermines the patriarchy. The philosophy underlying this conceptualization of the social movement is similar to what many feminists have referred to as cultural feminism (cf. Jaggar and Echols in Chapter 2).

Women's Equality. Within the Women's Equality ideology, the social problem of violence against women was defined as women's lack of power relative to men. More broadly, the problem was defined as one of power inequalities between oppressed and privileged social groups. The goal of the movement was conceptualized as the achievement of equal power between men and women, but the goal was often expanded to include equal power among all groups of people. The means to achieve this goal is through social and political change. This subcategory included some radical feminist ideas about changing sex-role practices and the economic value of women's reproductive work. However, liberal feminist ideas about achieving equal rights for women and other groups were offered most often. Most of the counselors advocated changes in the existing social and political system, to ensure better inclusion and protection of women, rather than a radical restructuring or abolition of the system itself.

Human Rights. Within the Human Rights ideology, the focus on oppressed groups shifted to a concern about individual problems and the social learning of violence. From this viewpoint, to reduce the exposure to violence and the opportunities for learning violence, we must control violence in the family and monitor violence in the media. We must protect victims through education and law enforcement. We must provide education and treatment for potential and actual abusers. We must pressure the media, both legislatively and economically, to produce and display less violence. These efforts are based in a philosophy of humanism, that is, the promotion of individual growth, the protection of individual rights, and the remediation of individual violators. Within this ideology, violence was described in gender-neutral terms: emerging out of families, affecting victims, perpetrated by abusers, and facilitated by the cultural desensitization to violence.

Having identified these three ideological sets with their underlying philosophies, I began to consider what had happened to the ideologies of the radical feminists who had been the impetus for the battered women's movement. It seemed to me that these radical ideologies had been diffused into the other philosophies that appeared to underlie the counselors' conceptualizations of the social movement in which they work. As a result, the ideology of radical feminism does not cohere in these battered women's programs as a guiding philosophy and program for change. Remnants of radical feminist philosophy can be found in the Women's

Affiliation ideology to the extent that building women's culture and alternative institutions is viewed as a revolutionary and political act. Elements of radical feminist beliefs can also be found in the Women's Equality ideology when some counselors suggest that the patriarchy must be overthrown, rather than modified to be more inclusive of women. Fragments of radical feminist ideas also can be found when, for example, counselors transcend the category of gender and analyze other social categories as oppressed.

The categories and subcategories that emerged do form a pattern of interconnectedness, as illustrated in Table 6.2. I should point out again that no individual counselor exactly fit any of the individual ideological sets. Rather, the counselors appear to jump around these categories when discussing the social movement. We saw earlier that this kind of conceptual shifting was also displayed by the participants when discussing counseling; however, there is some rationale for shifting conceptualizations in counseling when working with a variety of people with differing concerns. As long as one's approach within each conceptualization remains logically consistent, one's work with the client should not suffer. The problem is more acute when there is a lack of connectedness among problem definition, goals, and means of the social movement, because one's actions may run counter to the movement's ideal program for social change. There may be a disjunction between intent and action, between ends and means, that can impede progress toward change. Therefore, it became especially important for me, in my earlier study, to try to better understand the connections counselors made between their conceptions of the social movement and their counseling practice.

The Nexus of Ideology and Practice

Recall that the model derived from my research did not represent a single unified approach to counseling. Rather, it was a multilayered model in which the individual counselors appeared to shift their conceptualizations, depending on what seemed most salient for the client they were working with at a given point in counseling. Similarly, the model derived to describe how the social movement was construed by these counselors was also multilayered. Again, within this model, counselors seemed to shift between their conceptualizations so that it was difficult to pin down how any one counselor thought about the ideology. Moreover, there was a marked lack of theoretical coherence among concepts when counselors spoke about the movement's ideology.

My final research question referred to the ways in which counselors thought that the ideology of the movement affected or informed their counseling work. Having identified mixed models for both counseling and movement ideology, I initially wondered if it was still possible to say something about this nexus of ideology and practice. Counselors were not asked a direct question about how they thought the ideology of the movement influenced their counseling practice until very late in the interview. Nevertheless, because all the counselors acknowledged that they felt themselves to be part of a social movement, all of their responses up to that point can be seen as indicative of how they consider the nexus of ideology and counseling practice. It seemed to me that if the models that emerged out of this study were reflective of the counselors' conceptualizations of both counseling and the ideology of the social movement, then the influence (of ideology on counseling practice), however mixed, might be assessed by reference to the models.

In considering the question about the ways in which ideology informs counseling practice, one feature that stood out for me was the uniform denial by these counselors of a medical model influence. Illness concepts, symptom treatment, therapeutic interventions, therapist roles, and doctor-patient relationships were consciously and forcefully eschewed. Although I showed how illness concepts sometimes crept into the counselors' discussions, it was clear that these counselors tried to avoid illness terms in defining not only the problem of domestic violence but also the problems of the women who come to them for help. Certainly, this is one of the basic messages of the battered women movement: Women are not sick; (patriarchal) society is sick. Here, ideology has clearly influenced counseling conceptualizations of appropriate practice. Or, in this case, the ideology has called for the dismissal of a practice deemed inappropriate by the social movement: the medical model.

It was also my assessment that several subcategories of the political counseling submodel were not prominently used by these counselors. My overall impression was that despite the incisiveness of certain isolated sociopolitical analyses, the use of social action as a counseling technique, the role of the counselor as social activist *in the counseling sessions,* and the member-initiate aspects of the counselor-client relationship were minimized. This minimization was partly the result of a cautiousness on the part of counselors that they not impose their beliefs on the clients, that such imposition would be antithetical to an empowerment philosophy, and that commitments to social change are not for everyone. Some of the counselors approached a social action type of counseling when they emphasized the political nature of personal experiences, but they backed down before *imposing* that connection on their clients.

Once I had done this general analysis, I looked at the three ideological conceptualizations of the social movement and considered the counseling approaches that each seemed to emphasize. I analyzed that each of these ideological perspectives informed, in varying degrees, each of the first three counseling approaches: the resource, educational, and psychological approaches. Furthermore, two of the ideological sets minimally influenced concepts and strategies contained in the medical and political approaches.

Women's Affiliation and Counseling

The Women's Affiliation ideology views the social problem confronted by the battered women's movement as based in the devaluation of women in society. The movement goal is defined simply as the revaluation of women, and is best accomplished by women affiliating with each other to establish bonds and develop positive ideas of women. This sort of ideology, which has some affinities with cultural feminist beliefs, most strongly influences the resource and psychological approaches to counseling. The ideology informs the resource approach by suggesting that the most important counseling goal, like the primary goal of the movement, is survival (of the battered woman, of the movement itself). It informs the psychological approach through its emphasis on women's mutual affiliation and its individualized focus on healing and empowerment of women by women. To a lesser extent, the women's affiliation ideology could be said to inform the educational counseling approach by emphasizing women's need for an alternative education about the value of women.

Women's Equality and Counseling

The Women's Equality ideology suggests that the problem in society is that women as a group lack power relative to men. In addition, other oppressed groups lack power relative to more privileged groups. The goal of the battered women's movement from this perspective is to create a society in which men and women, gays and lesbians, people of color and whites—all peoples—have equal power. To accomplish this goal, workers in the movement promote changes at the societal level that will recognize and equalize the rights, opportunities, and economic status of women and other oppressed groups. But counselors, who work at the individual level, stay focused on the notion that the personal is political and so help individual women achieve their rights and get free from abuse. In addition, counselors sometimes acknowledge that abused women might feel better (more empowered) when they become involved in political work, so they occasionally provide opportunities for battered women to participate in political action when they can ethically justify that they are not imposing their own values on the woman.

The analysis of the Women's Equality ideology moves from the political to the individual and back again. It has a number of potential implications for counseling approaches. This ideology informs the resource approach by viewing the survival of individual women, who become empowered to obtain the resources for survival, as aggregating into the development of a society that does not abuse women. The ideology strongly affects the educational approach, in which social structural change toward women's equality is viewed largely as based in reeducating people and changing attitudes. To a lesser extent, the women's equality ideology informs the psychological counseling approach, which emphasizes women's relational experiences with one another. Women valuing one another, women being together, women helping one another are all political statements and efforts, even when they might not appear so to the individual woman. Again, the personal is political. Finally, within this ideological conceptualization, there appears some influence on the use of a political counseling approach. Political counseling was approximated by some counselors as they consciously considered the political aspects of personal experience. None of these counselors, however, identified social action as an integral part of an abused woman's healing, as it is identified in PCADV's Program Model.

Human Rights and Counseling

The counselors who employed humanistic concepts and a Human Rights ideology did identify the need for social change in the way violence is both tolerated and promoted in our culture, but they employed a gender-neutral analysis to emphasize that violence is learned by individuals through exposure to violence. Such an ideology informs, to some degree, both the educational and the psychological counseling approaches. Within the educational approach, it is seen as necessary to educate people about the inappropriateness of violence. Those who are abused must be taught that they should not tolerate abuse. Those who abuse must learn to respect the rights of others. In counseling, we will reeducate people regarding their false beliefs. From the perspective of the human rights ideology, when violence occurs, we look for individual psychological explanations based in theories about the effects of exposure to violence. This ideology also influences the psychological approach to counseling in battered women's programs. Counselors working with battered women offer a relationship that provides an opportunity for relearning so that individual women will no longer tolerate violence in their relationships.

To a lesser extent, the humanist ideology informs the resource counseling approach by emphasizing that when violence does occur, because one person is not respecting the rights of another, it is important to help the victim get free from the abuser. Finally, this humanistic perspective also has a minimal effect on the illness approach to counseling. Because we as a society and as individuals are not yet at a point where we do not see difference, there are some people who do not respect the rights of others, and there are other people who allow themselves to be victimized. This is certainly a matter of individual pathology on the part of the abuser and sometimes on the part of the victim. When it is a matter of pathology, we must provide counseling that heals the illness and treats the symptoms. Counseling should be directed at both the abuser and the victim.

Overall, I am suggesting that the influence of ideology on the counseling approaches is mixed, but that some social movement conceptualizations appear to more strongly inform some counseling approaches than others. Moreover, although the actual ideology of the battered women's movement does employ a sociopolitical analysis, and the PCADV does encourage social action as a part of empowerment counseling, these counselors who work in Pennsylvania programs have not fully incorporated social action as a counseling practice.

Counseling:
A Conservative or Subversive Activity?

My original framework suggested that counseling might be either conserving or subverting in its goals. Counseling might serve to help people adjust to the status quo, or it might help people challenge the situations, the institutions, the attitudes that fostered the problem confronting them. Though this framework proved to be oversimplified, I still thought it useful to consider broadly whether the counseling practice in Pennsylvania battered women's programs was conservative or subversive in nature.

First, I considered the denial of illness concepts for the (women) victims of domestic violence and sexual assault. Women are not sick, yet they have gotten the message that they are sick because they have been abused. That message has come from the abuser, from family, from the media, from our culture. The counterbalancing message from these counselors was that society is sick, the culture has provided incorrect information, people's attitudes are misinformed, the victim is not to blame for the abuse. Certainly, this is a "subversive" message in its assertion that the status quo is problematic. But the message can also be victim blaming if it goes no further or if its counseling activities are directed toward changes in individual understanding, rather than toward challenging and changing the social system. The victim hears, "Everything you've learned up to date is incorrect. It's not your fault, but it's time for reeducation." The implication is that once women have this new information, they will manage to stop being abused. But such a position does not fundamentally challenge the social system. Perhaps, if enough people learn and accept the new information, they might be mobilized to make systemic changes. These counselors, however, stop short of recruiting women into a social movement that does challenge and work for changes in the system.

The human rights ideological perspective promotes a focus on individual problems and individual solutions. In counseling, this goal is furthered by providing alternative education (about individual rights) and relational experiences that are personally empowering. Apart from helping individuals, the only social change advocated by the human rights ideology is the reduction of cultural violence in the media. If there is any common strategy among humanists, it is the solid belief in individual change and legislative protection as the keys to the amelioration of social problems. An amended version of this stance has been adopted by some

New Age philosophers who urge individuals to change their own reality—that is, their perception of reality—rather than trying to change the actual external circumstances.[1] In effect, such a position works to conserve the status quo of society by implying that the basic need of the client is to change only her perception of how society affects her.

The women's affiliation ideology promotes a world in which women are valued. In such a world, women have equal access to participation in society but remain essentially different from men—different, but valued equally. The primary strategies of such a movement are promoting women's affiliation with one another and building a community based in women's values. Less overtly, this ideology also supports a kind of separatism, based on a separate (different) but equal doctrine. In counseling, these strategies inform the resource and psychological submodels. Individual women must survive abuse and violence and must learn to relate to and value women as a group.

The question of whether women's affiliation and culture building can be considered subversive to the existing social and political system is a complex one. Certainly, separatism and building alternative institutions have been considered subversive activities by many feminists who identify themselves as radical or cultural feminists. But the ultimate test of the effectiveness of a strategy is to assume its success and then consider its results. Unfortunately, the successful creation of a separate women's community does not guarantee equality of rights and power among men and women in the larger society. In my opinion, the women's affiliation ideology and the counseling strategies that promote affiliation as a goal in and of itself cannot be considered politically subversive.

The women's equality ideology promotes not only equality of rights and power between men and women but also the elimination of oppressed and privileged power groups. It articulates social action strategies (e.g. demonstrations, legislative change) that confront, challenge, counter, and shift power structures. Its counseling strategies include efforts to achieve individual rights, as in the resource approach; reeducation about women's rights and roles, as in the educational approach; and attempts to change attitudes about women, as in the psychological approach. Both the ideological perspective and the counseling effort make a conscious connection between the personal and the political. Together, these might seem subversive to the existing system in that they promote a new social order and suggest personal and political strategies to achieve that order. But, as discussed above, the actual counseling usually stops short of incorporating specific social action strategies into the counseling sessions and remains focused on individual remediation.

Clearly, there were both confusion and conflict in the counselors' thinking about the need for social change for women as a group and the need for social change for all oppressed peoples. In part, the conflict arises out of attempts to respond to the needs and criticisms of particular groups of women—women of color who have felt the white women's movement does not take their experience into account; lesbians who feel they must remain invisible or at least quiet within a heterosexist women's movement; women of lower socioeconomic class who have not had access to higher education, unlike their professionally trained sisters; women of differing physical ability who do not have physical access to the meeting places of an able-bodied women's movement. The ideological attempt to respond to the differential needs of these women and the recognition that it is not only women who experience racism, homophobia, classism, and ableism led to some questions about whether to pursue feminist goals for equality between men and women or socialist goals for equality among all groups and every individual. A similar conflict divided those women who identified as radical feminists and those who identified as politicos or socialist feminists in the 1960s and 1970s. The question became, is the sex-class system or the socioeconomic class division the fundamental source of oppression? Or is race, perhaps, the fundamental issue? These distinctions were not clearly articulated in the conceptualizations of counselors in this study. As a result, they offered an idealized expression that there will be no perceived differences at all in our future society.

Unquestionably, the ways in which the ideology of the social movement is conceptualized influence counseling practice. That influence was not consistent, however, because of the confusion about ideology and the conflict between ideologies that the counselors in my study tried to hold simultaneously. A few counselors viewed themselves and their work as subversive, that is, challenging the power structures of patriarchal society. Most viewed themselves and their work as idealistic, that is, promoting an ideal (largely through individual education) of societal homogenization and equality without taking political action.

Historically, the nature of counseling has been to focus on the individual and the problems she brings to the counseling session to discuss. The function of counseling has been to help that individual. Even when a counselor is aware of the social context of problems and promotes an understanding of that context in counseling, the focus has remained on the individual. But I believe that when the individual's problems are primarily rooted in society, counseling must include a political component. The counselors in my study did work to ensure that women were informed of and could access their legal rights. Most of the counselors viewed part of their role as engaging in social change activities. They failed, however, to advocate strongly for women to join them in challenging institutionalized power and, to that extent, they remained focused on remediating the individual problems of individual women. This type of counseling activity may be conserving in helping women adjust to their situations, or it may be subversive in helping a particular woman challenge and change her situation, but it remains an individualized and incremental approach to social change.

I found myself, at this point, questioning the practice of counseling in these social movement programs. The counselors I interviewed believed that their counseling practice was radically different from traditional counseling in that it challenged the status quo. Certainly, they wanted a better world for women—and for other oppressed peoples. I was concerned, however, about the ways in which the counseling activity itself promoted or failed to promote this better world. Surely, many individual women have been helped, through these counseling efforts, to get out of abusive relationships, to heal from previous abuse. But are these women encouraged to look for ways to prevent the future abuse of other women? Based on my interviews with the counselors who participated in this study, the answer to that question was no. I found that answer disheartening. For as much as I admired the dedicated assistance these counselors have provided individual abused women, I believe counseling has a role to play in rooting out the societal sources of abuse. The original ideas and rationale for that aspect of the role of counseling are articulated in the radical therapy literature and in the PCADV Program Model, but these theories need further development. I hold that it would invigorate the counseling efforts in these feminist social movement programs to reincorporate that social change emphasis. Ultimately, it is this social action component that can truly differentiate subversive from conservative counseling. So now I offer a model that I believe will accomplish this goal.

Note

1. New Age philosophy has much broader parameters than the focus on changing one's perception of reality. Still, this issue has been singled out for criticism by the battered women's movement (Freechild, 1989).

Counseling to
End Woman Battering

My research had led me to the conclusion that the counselors I interviewed did not have a coherent understanding of the ideological foundations that informed their counseling practice. But a lack of ideological coherence was less disturbing for me than the fact that the primary ideology that influenced their counseling models and practices was not the social change ideology of the battered women's movement. Instead, those models and practices were based on their understanding of the role of counseling in helping individual battered women get free from their abusive relationships. As a result, these counselors were effectively able to separate their counseling practice from whatever political activities they thought appropriate to engage in. I am still puzzling over finding this kind of compartmentalization within a radical feminist social change movement. Why, in a state like Pennsylvania, with a domestic violence coalition that has a strong feminist orientation and an established feminist model of collective empowerment, would I find these disjunctures between political activism and counseling, between collective power strategies and individual empowerment? I need to suggest some tentative answers to this conundrum before proposing a counseling model that I think improves upon the model PCADV already has.

The Separation of
Counseling and Social Change

One potential source for this compartmentalization lies in the training curriculum for counselors and volunteers in battered women's programs. In most U.S. programs that are part of statewide domestic violence coalitions, counselors, volunteers, and often other program staff undergo some kind of training by the program. In Pennsylvania, that training is mandated by law for all program workers and is tied not only to program standards, which are monitored by the coalition, but also to the confidentiality statutes, which grant that any communication between a battered woman client and a domestic violence counselor is privileged. The training curriculum, originally developed by individual programs and shared with new programs as they emerged, was eventually compiled and reworked by PCADV and is now mandated for all programs. The curriculum includes an analysis of the problem of violence against women and offers a Feminist Empowerment Model as the rubric under which all services to battered women are to be offered. Another of the training components involves learning about, practicing, and developing empowerment counseling skills; that is, developing the interpersonal skills needed to empathically listen and respond to women in crisis.

Each program has a fair amount of latitude in developing and delivering its training program as long as it addresses all the curricular components mandated by PCADV. So, one possible answer to the question of compartmentalization is that individual programs are not doing an adequate job of integrating the curricular components of the training, either because the training staff, supervisors, administrators, and boards of directors, either separately or together, don't fully understand its integration or because they don't believe in all of its premises. Consequently, these components are taught separately, given differing emphases, and internalized by the trainees compartmentally. This explanation seems to fit my experience in conducting the interviews.

There are two other issues related to this matter of a curriculum that separates components of training into distinct sessions. The first issue involves the way in which basic counseling skills can be implemented within a counseling model that privileges social change activities on the part of the client. The second issue returns to the question of empowerment as a concept.

Workers in battered women's programs, like most counselors and psychologists trained professionally in schools of higher education, are first taught Rogerian-style listening and responding skills. We are taught that the first order of business in any therapeutic endeavor is to establish a connection, a relationship with the client. We listen, we paraphrase, we empathize, we indicate our understanding. We seek points of connection with the client, no matter how abhorrent or strange his or her behavior might be, so that we can understand the client's worldview, how it developed, and what points will provide the best sites for the fulcrum of change for that individual. This emphasis on connecting with the individual client can easily be misinterpreted as the goal, rather than a means, of counseling. Still, I continue to think that these skills, these connections, are central to the counseling endeavor. But both the failure to ground those skills in a ideology that focuses on social change and the failure to connect them to a model that incorporates social change activities result in a counseling practice that is limited to relating to the individual. I am proposing that our skills be directed in the service of a somewhat different goal. That is, instead of being focused on helping the individual client who is sitting in our office, our goal ought to be conceptualized as changing the world in line with our vision. Or, as Laura Brown (1994) puts it, the primary client of the radical feminist counselor is the culture.

The second issue that needs revisitation is the concept of empowerment. In Chapter 3, I reviewed some feminist criticisms of empowerment as a problematic construct that implies one person—the counselor—giving power to another—the client. These critics believe empowerment implies an inegalitarian relationship between counselor and client, something that should be avoided in feminist counseling practice. However, I am willing to acknowledge that the counselor holds more power in the counseling relationship than does the client. I believe the counselor can use that asymmetry of power to provide the client with information and tactics to get the client's needs met. I happen to believe empowerment is an effective strategy—at the individual level. But that is also its limitation. When empowerment strategies are used to help an individual woman understand her unique situational complexities, identify goals for changing her situation, and develop resources to implement goals, these strategies can help individual women get free. At the same time, however, these empowerment strategies reinforce the perception that this woman's battering is an individual situation that demands individual changes. I believe that empowerment strategies need to be supplemented with strategies aimed at helping women practice power and seize power, and these latter strategies must be used in the service of understanding woman battering as a social problem that requires collective solutions.

A Vision of Equality

To ensure that our counseling practice is in line with our vision of social change, we must first articulate that vision and be clear about where we are headed and how to get there. As a feminist who is particularly concerned about the condition of women in our society, my vision involves making the world a better place for women. I envision a world, a society, in which women and men participate in both public and domestic spheres, sharing responsibilities and rewards equally. I envision a partnership between men and women of all colors, sexualities, and physical abilities, a partnership in which the work of society and the work of the home are accomplished together; a partnership built on mutual respect, concern, and care, rather than hatred, terror, self-interest, and appropriation; a partnership in which all groups want to participate and all groups are welcomed, rather than some groups being coerced into or excluded from participation. Some of these partnerships will take the form of a deeper love and include expressions of sexuality and perhaps commitments to relationships, or bearing and raising children. But each party in the relationship will come with the skills, the confidence, and sufficient concern for the other that neither will overpower the other. This is a world in which women will not be singled out by men for abuse, violence, and the threat of violence.

This vision is an expression of an ideology about the proper relationship between men and women and the construction of a just and caring society. Using the terms of the model framed through my case study, I would call the social movement organized to achieve this vision a movement to end violence against women. This movement includes a more specific battered women's movement aimed at ending violence against women in intimate relationships. Although I will later suggest implications of this vision and my counseling model for people in a wide variety of circumstances who are oppressed by the social conditions in which they live, my primary concern in this book is the social problem of woman battering. Therefore, I intend to concentrate here on the ideological and counseling models that I believe are appropriate for working with battered women.

An Ideological Model for Social Change

A subversive, radical feminist counseling practice needs to be grounded in a coherent social change ideological model, so I will first frame a social change model for counselors who work with battered women. This model is not intended to reflect every nuance of the radical feminist ideology of the battered women's movement. Rather, it is meant to be a simplified statement of some of its essential components: its problem statement, its goals, the means necessary to accomplish the goals, its guiding philosophy. In presenting my summary, I will use universal terms like *men* or *women* when describing the model. Clearly, there are men who support the goals of the battered women's movement and there are women who oppose those goals. But ideologies are usually grounded in an understanding of history in its broadest identification of the loci of power and powerlessness. Therefore, I will present a summary of the radical feminist ideology in its most general form. I believe that if counselors can grasp this simplified model and become able to articulate this ideology, they will be able to begin grounding their counseling practice in conceptualizations of social change rather than individual change. Figure 7.1 depicts this social change framework for ending male violence against women.

Problem Definition:
Male Violence Against Women

Simply stated, the social problem that contemporary feminist social movements confront is that women in our society are socially and politically controlled by men; that is, women are oppressed. Social and political

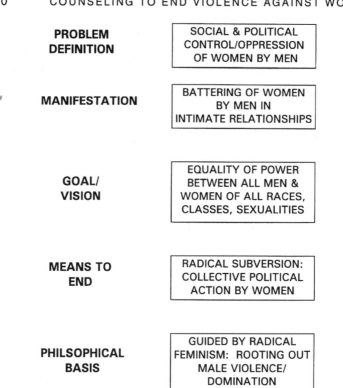

Figure 7.1. A Social Change Framework for Ending Male Violence Against Women

control is frequently manifested through male violence against women, and one specific manifestation of the problem is that women are battered by men in their intimate relationships. According to the ideological analysis offered by the movement, men batter the women they supposedly love because they benefit from such abuse, both individually and collectively. We live in a patriarchal society that has promoted and supported male domination over women: male authority, male power, male control. In such a society, men as a group have benefited materially from domination by accumulating and controlling whatever economic resources were available within their class and racial groupings. They have solidified their economic power by controlling the political process and occupying positions of political power in government and in business. At times, they have benefited by their use of women as a free labor force in the home, and as a cheap labor source in the marketplace. Men as a group have also benefited psychologically from their domination of women. Men perceive themselves as better than women: stronger, more intelligent, more capable of controlling economic resources, more able as citizens and leaders. The result is a mass psychological feeling of powerfulness in men, in relation to women. Even when some groups of men experience feelings of powerlessness in relation to other groups of men, they can still experience a modicum of powerful feelings in relation to women. Women are always subject to the control of men, and women accommodate their behavior to mollify men and avoid the extremes of men's exertions of power. They marry, they become dutiful subjects, they cajole, they nurture, and they enjoy the few privileges they are permitted. These behaviors become defined as "women's nature."

These examples of the ways in which men benefit at a societal level from male domination have a parallel in individual male-female intimate relationships. Many men benefit materially from the exertion of power in their heterosexual relationships. It is the man who typically controls the economic resources of the household and can use those resources in whatever ways he determines. It is the man who is the designated head of the household, and decisions about the family ultimately rest with him. Individual men benefit psychologically from this arrangement by feeling powerful and exerting power over the women in their lives. They benefit from women's accommodation to this situation and women's behaviors that are directed toward loving, admiring, nurturing, and humoring the person in control. For the man who batters, the benefits are more direct. The batterer can control the economic resources of the household, feel the psychological benefits of power, and ensure behaviors from the woman that attempt to avoid further abuse. So the patriarchal society that structures and perpetuates male domination filters down to the level of individual intimate relationships and is especially reflected in physically abusive relationships. These abusive relationships, in turn, reinforce the structure of heterosexual relationships in general and ultimately re-create and support patriarchal society.

Movement Goals: Equal Power and Nonviolence

The vision of the movement, as I described earlier, is a utopian world in which all groups have equal power, resources, responsibilities, and access to opportunities. It is a world in which the power is not concentrated in the hands of a few, so there is no oppression on the basis of group identity by gender, race, or sexuality. There are no less privileged groups. Therefore, women as a group are not oppressed; there is no violence directed at women as a group in an effort to keep them in their oppressed place. There is no battering in intimate relationships, because relationships are based in social equality, mutual trust, and caring. In this world, society may still be confronted with individual acts of violence, but it will not be violence of one group of people aimed at another group of people because of some category of gender or race or sexuality.

The Means: Revolutionary Transformation

Within the framework of this ideological model, the means to achieve this vision involves a radical restructuring of our social and political system. It is insufficient to try making a series of minor reforms to this system. In the present system, the wealth is concentrated in the hands of a few; we are governed by and programs are administered predominantly by white males; values of competition and materialism predominate; we promote independence, individualism, and manipulation at the expense of interdependence, empathy, and caring. Yet, a violent revolution is antithetical to the vision of a violence-free world. Therefore, we must think in terms of revolutionary but nonviolent transformation. Women must join together to take radical, transformative political action, and through their collective strength women will attain more power.

Philosophy: Radical Feminism

Radical feminism is the philosophy that guides this vision, its goals and means. This is a radical feminism that seeks to eradicate the root causes of sexism, racism, homophobia, ageism, and ableism. It is a radical feminism that attends to the differences among us but values understanding and appreciation of difference while seeking coalitions for change. Within the battered women's movement, the philosophy of radical feminism acknowledges the reality that any woman may be battered, regardless of race, social class, or sexual orientation. It acknowledges that women are oppressed and violated not only by sexism but also by racism, classism, ableism, heterosexism, and ageism. It promotes the notion of building coalitions among diverse groups of women, in the service of creating a world free of violence directed at women.

Connecting Counseling to our Social Vision

I concede that the ideology I've outlined is idealized and simplified. It does not respond to all the questions about women's inequality and oppression, nor does it suggest solutions to all the problems, but it does provide a coherent basis from which to build a counseling model that promotes social change in line with this radical feminist vision. If one is a psychologist or counselor who works within a battered women's movement, or whose primary responsibilities are counseling battered women, the question becomes how best to further one's vision of a world free of violence against women. Some have argued that the practice of psychology is antithetical to the work of collective social change. If this argument is valid, then one's counseling efforts are necessarily separate from any efforts to change the social context in which client lives are lived. One's life and work become cordoned off into distinct spheres: Here I will help an individual feel better; here I will participate in political action to change the system. As we have seen, my case study revealed that counselors in battered women's programs do compartmentalize their efforts in this way. But I reject this compartmentalization of counseling and political action, and I remain hopeful of achieving an integration of these actions within this model. Figure 7.2 provides a graphic representation of this subversive counseling model.

A Subversive Counseling Model

I am going to frame a counseling model that meets these criteria through the theoretical categories of understanding that emerged from my case study research. That is, the primary categories of Women's Problems, Women's Needs, Counseling Interventions, Counselor Role, and Counselor-Client Relationship have construct validity and can be filled out within an approach to counseling as a subversive activity.

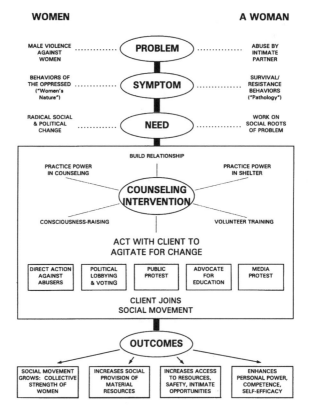

Figure 7.2. Subversive Counseling Model

Women's Problems: Behaviors of Survival and Resistance

The roots of women's problems, and battered women's problems in particular, lie in our male-dominated society. The oppression of women by men results in predictable "symptomatic" behaviors. Women, in general, manifest a variety of behaviors that are consistent with getting along in a society in which they have relatively little power. These behaviors become thought of as "women's nature." For battered women coping with ongoing abuse by an intimate partner, the behaviors of survival and resistance are often labeled "pathological." Within our counseling model, therefore, we must view Women's Problems and "symptoms," as experienced within the context of a battering relationship, by starting with respect for battered women. This comment is not meant as a platitude but as an integral part of the counseling model. That is, we need to respect battered women as people who are struggling as best they can against a victimization and oppression that is rooted in society. We need to assume that battered women do not want to be battered and do not want their children to be affected by this violence. As counselors and psychologists, we need to work to understand the behaviors we see battered women engaging in as survival and coping behaviors rather than indicators of psychological illness. If we see battered women returning time and again to their battering relationship, expressing their love for their batterer, we need to understand the very limited resources and opportunities available to women, rather than analyzing these behaviors as masochistic, self-defeating, learned helplessness, or Stockholm syndrome. If we see battered women indecisive, anxious, morose, lethargic, and lacking confidence, then instead of diagnosing them with PTSD, we need to understand how these behaviors might serve to protect them from additional abuse. If we see battered women abusing their own children or putting them in harm's way, then instead of analyzing this behavior as displacement, scapegoating, or irresponsible, we need to understand how these behaviors might safeguard the children and the battered woman from even more extreme violence by the abuser. I am not suggesting that these interpretations of behaviors are the "correct" understandings. I am only suggesting that our efforts be directed initially toward an understanding of behavior as coping and survival techniques, rather than toward diagnosing an inherent pathology or the pathological effects of battering.

Women's Needs: Political and Social Change

As we work to understand and define battered women's problems as a means of coping and surviving, we begin to see more clearly Women's Needs. Battered women need information about the limited protections currently available to them. They need to know about those protections and about the serious limitations of the legal system in safeguarding them from further abuse and violence. As counselors and psychologists, we need to take seriously the battered woman's fear that she and her children might be killed if she tries to leave. It is all too easy to tell battered women that statistically a small number of abusers actually follow through on their threats about what they will do if their partners leave. It really doesn't matter how small that number is. Why would any battered woman want to risk, and why should we expect her to risk, her life or the lives of her children to get away?

What battered women need in order to get away from the battering relationship are material resources. Initially, they need a safe place, a secure shelter, from which to gather what material resources they can—from their homes, from their partners, from their bank accounts, from their marital assets, and from the state. When there are limited material resources in the family or when they cannot be accessed, as is often the case, battered women need additional resources from the state. They need housing, food, clothing, and money. They may need education and job training. They may need to relocate and retain anonymity from their abusive partners. They may need legal divorces. They may need access to jobs and child care. These are resources that could be provided by a just and caring government that operates to protect and provide for its citizens, a government that ensures equal opportunity in the job market by providing equal education, pay equity, and child care. The creation of this kind of government calls for social and political change.

But battered women, though they need these material resources at a minimum, need more. Few battered women want to spend their lives in isolation, cut off from intimate, loving relationships. It is often this fear that leads them to stay in abusive relationships. Relationships with children and coworkers are insufficient to satisfy most women's needs for connection with a partner in life. Thus, battered women also need opportunities for connection, for sharing, for respecting and being respected, for trusting and being trusted, for loving and being loved. Clearly, these are opportunities that a state cannot mandate, so political actions and policy changes for love and connection opportunities do not seem feasible. These are needs felt by many people, men and women, and if one is not currently "hooked up" with someone, he or she confronts some real dilemmas and dangers about meeting and connecting with potential partners. What is needed is more fundamental, broad-based social change in our attitudes and conceptualizations of women, relationship, and sexuality.

So, if battered women's problems are defined as coping behaviors that aid in their survival, then their needs are for information and resources, for political changes that will provide more resources and improved access to opportunities, and for social changes that will result in attitudes of respect for women as equal partners. From this perspective, battered women's needs are not for healing, but for acting; not for empowerment, but for seizing power; not for independence, but for connection on the basis of equality. It is these behaviors—social action, seizing power, connecting—that can act on the social sources of inequality and battering. Moreover, acting on these social sources has individual effects as well for the actor. That is, as we seek to meet women's collective needs for political action, for taking power, and for equality, we engage individual battered women in a parallel process by which they concomitantly heal, feel empowered, and become more independent.

Counseling Interventions: Joining for Social Action

Now we can consider what counseling can offer to help meet these needs. My proposal is that the counseling interventions that are consistent with these definitions of the problems and needs of battered women are those that incorporate social change activities into the counseling effort. I will be writing as if both counselor and client are women, though the model has more general applicability and can be used by both male and female counselors, an extrapolation I will explore later. But because here I am contextualizing the model for use within battered women's programs, a gender-specific model is appropriate. Within the context of the social problem of woman battering, some points of connection are more easily made on the basis of a shared identification as women. In most battered women's programs and shelters, almost all of the staff and volunteers are women, so my discussion reflects that reality and builds on the interpersonal and political implications of women helping women.

Relationship Building. I reiterate my acknowledgment of the importance of some basic counseling skills to build a connection between client and counselor. As counselors for battered women, we must be able to listen and respond to women's concerns, their fears, their particular needs and desires. We listen from a framework that does not pathologize their behavior and thoughts. We respond as women who can empathize with the situation they confront, validating their experience and their reality. We listen as people who care about women in our society; we respond with care for them as women. We are firm within our own self-concepts of woman; we have developed a love of ourselves as women, and by our presentation of ourselves, we communicate that approval, love, and respect for women. In this manner, we build a connection and relationship with the woman client, as women.

It is critical to stress this relationship-building process, which I believe is essential to any counseling endeavor, because the social change activities I propose should not be interpreted as a manipulative effort to get the client to follow the counselor's political agenda. Feminist psychologists began their critique of traditional psychotherapy by noting that no therapeutic endeavor is value free. The problem with traditional psychotherapy was that it purported to be value-neutral while promoting client adjustment to the social and political status quo. Feminist psychologists argued that it was an ethical responsibility to make explicit the values that guided one's therapeutic approach so that the client could be free to accept or reject those values. I am arguing that the values that radical feminist counselors ought to hold include their affirmation of social change activities as a positive part of the counseling endeavor. We build a relationship with the client while making those values explicit. We talk about the ways in which social change activities connect not only to the larger societal problem of violence against women but also to the individual's personal life. If a counselor fails to establish a caring relationship as a base, few clients would listen, trust, believe, or take action on the opportunities the counselor might make available to them. I believe that these basic counseling skills and the establishment of a relationship should be in the service of women as a group connecting for broader social change, rather than two women connecting for one woman's individual change. What women need, what battered women need, are material resources and social changes, not merely changes in the way they perceive and cope with their particular situations.

Consciousness-Raising. Once this relationship is established, how does one go about incorporating social change activities into the counseling sessions? In most instances, one of the preliminary activities that a counselor engages in with a battered woman is consciousness-raising; however, it is important to be clear that this must be a consciousness-raising that is directed toward the activity of social change. Recall that early feminist therapists emphasized the use of consciousness-raising in therapy sessions. This emphasis led to not only an intense debate among women's liberation groups over the role of consciousness-raising in women's groups but also the concern that consciousness-raising could devolve into individual self-absorption without leading to action.

So consciousness-raising, which for the early women's liberation movement meant identifying commonalities in our experiences as women and understanding the political implications of those commonalities, must be a carefully monitored counseling intervention. The danger is that it can promote self-reflection and self-realization and not result in making the connection from the personal to the political, from narcissistic thought to collective action. But if the goal of connecting personal experience to collective analysis to political action is kept in mind, consciousness-raising can serve to promote reinterpretations of behaviors and revaluations of women while nurturing women's identification with women as a group. Consciousness-raising, when it initiates a "click" of realization in one woman's mind, promotes connections among women by providing them a clear identification of the battered woman's problem as a social problem. It is this connection that supports social and political change activities.

Collective Power in Shelter. Another form of social change activity, which has the potential for becoming part of the counseling intervention, is possible when battered women come to stay in a battered women's shelter for a period of time. In a shelter that is operated under a philosophy of collective empowerment, battered women are given the responsibility and opportunity to take part in the decision making about the operation of the shelter. There are a variety of means for doing this: having shelter residents attend staff meetings, raising concerns and problems that affect the daily living in shelter activities, promoting and supporting resident decisions about those activities. If the shelter program is truly committed to a collective work structure and the sharing of power among all the people involved, the voice and participation of shelter residents may be welcomed and responded to. Such activities provide the opportunity for battered women to engage in the practice of political action in a microcosmic environment. Unfortunately, the time limitations on the length of stay permitted for each woman make it difficult to bring this activity to its potential fruition. By the time a battered woman has moved into the shelter and begun to consider what she will do next and how she will do it, it may be time to leave the shelter. And it must also be admitted that few shelter programs aspire to this collective work structure or the full inclusion of battered women in the decision making; and when they do so aspire, fewer still are able to achieve either the collective ideal or the inclusion of battered women, because of the constraints of funding sources or boards of directors. This dilemma points to the importance of connecting ideology to both organizational structure and counseling practice. The issue of organizational structure is beyond the scope of this book and has been covered adequately by others (Gornick, Burt, & Pittman, 1983; PCADV, 1987; Schechter, 1982). I note it here not only because of the potential for practicing power within a collectively organized shelter but also to recognize the limits of the real situation in most battered women's programs.

Volunteer Training. One type of social change activity that many battered women's programs have somewhat more successfully incorporated into counseling is encouraging battered women clients to partake in the volunteer training of the program. The first step for an individual's becoming part of the battered women's movement is often this experience of volunteer training. The training curriculum reinforces the insights and consciousness-raising offered in counseling. If the battered woman, subsequent to the training, decides to volunteer for the program in some way (staffing the hotline, responding to crisis calls, assisting in the shelter, providing educational programs), she has in effect joined the movement.

When battered women join the movement, there are multidimensional benefits. There are benefits to the individual woman, who gains a sense of connection and affiliation with a larger group of women working collectively on a broader goal. There is the sense of relief that comes from understanding that one's individual situation is a reflection of a larger social problem and that the way to address the problem is by addressing the social issue. This tactic focuses the individual on attacking the social roots of the problem and relieves her of responsibility for changing her individual situation. There is a sense of self-efficacy that comes from taking political action, from practicing power, and from helping other battered women join the movement. Going beyond the benefits to the individual battered woman, there is the benefit of increasing numbers of women joined together to effect social and political change. Moreover, encouraging battered women to become program volunteers is an essential first step in creating and maintaining a battered women's movement that is a movement of and for battered women, reflective of and responsive to the needs of battered women.

Direct Actions Against the Abuser. Despite the beneficial effects, both collective and individual, of battered women joining the movement, social change activities in counseling need not be put on hold until the battered woman goes through volunteer training. Some women's groups have been successful at initiating direct actions against abusers as a way of publicizing and punishing an individual man's violence against a woman. Such actions, when the battered woman is included in the planning and implementation, may also be seen as a counseling effort that incorporates social change activity. For instance, in South America, women's groups have painted signs on the batterer's house, denouncing his behavior and holding him up for censure by the community. In the United States, given our basic beliefs in constitutional guarantees of innocence until proof of guilt, we tend to think it inappropriate and perhaps illegal to engage in this kind of direct confrontation; however, finding ways to publicize domestic disturbance calls to the police, or protection orders that have been issued by a court, or alleged battering or court findings of battering can contribute to public identification of a situation that the batterer is usually eager to keep private.

For example, if the national press had picked up on the many police calls made by Nicole Brown over the years, and had publicized them each time she was threatened and beaten or allegedly threatened and beaten, public censure would have been brought to bear on O. J. Simpson long before her murder. It is possible that making his behavior public could have exerted public pressure on his corporate sponsors, thus affecting his earnings. It is possible that public censure, resulting from public exposure of his behavior, would have raised questions long ago about O. J.'s image as an admirable sports and media hero. Therefore, he would have experienced pressures to alter his behavior. I am not trying to say that the murder of Nicole Brown would have been avoided, for that cannot be known with certainty. In fact, it is possible that his violence would have escalated in an attempt to terrorize Nicole Brown from making further reports. But the likelihood is that, by forcing the abuse out of the privacy of the home, public censure would have forced him to curtail his threats and his violence.

The example of O. J. Simpson is relevant for nationally known figures, but a similar principle can also be applied in smaller communities. In very small communities and midsize communities, the lives of batterers can be negatively affected by more public disclosure about battering incidents.

Employment, friendships, and community contacts can all be affected if a batterer's behavior is made public. Moreover, by publicizing a particular batterer's behavior, in cooperation with a battered woman client, other battered women may discover sources of support they did not know existed, including battered women's programs, feminist counseling, and a women's community that refuses to tolerate violence against women. In short, whether the batterer is nationally known or known only within a smaller community, direct actions that make public the person's behavior might be an effective means of preventing future violence and possibly helping battered women get free. Although battered women's programs might not want to risk legal action by publicly denouncing battering behavior when it has not yet been proved, or might not want to risk personal endangerment or retaliation by an angry batterer, I believe battered women's programs and counselors could be a source of creative ideas about direct actions that do not violate our laws or exacerbate a batterer's violence. Such actions, when initiated as part of counseling, should be undertaken only with the full involvement of the battered woman. This involvement is an essential consideration for this counseling model and its emphasis on helping the individual woman through engaging her in social action strategies. Like any social action made part of counseling, direct actions are to be understood as working on the root of the problem. The individual's problem is battering, a problem rooted in society; the personal is political. Actions against a particular abuser make public the social problem of battering and so contribute to the eventual eradication of battering.

Political Actions. A somewhat more obvious way to engage battered women in direct action is through public challenges to the political and cultural power structures. These actions could come from a radical or a liberal feminist analysis. On the political front, feminist groups in the United States have a history of taking public action against institutions. We have organized demonstrations and picket lines. We have testified in public hearings and held public speak-outs about battering. At times, we have demonstrated against individual representatives of institutions, denouncing the decisions of certain judges, law enforcement officers, administrators of public programs. We have lobbied our legislators, at the state and national level, to initiate legal and policy changes that would ease the burden on battered women. All of these are social change activities that can include the participation of the battered woman client, and can therefore become part of the counseling intervention itself when the counselor joins with the battered woman in taking such action.

Social and Cultural Actions. Challenges to cultural practices and understandings are harder to target because of the difficulty in making decisions about where best to intervene for change. It is within this area that more fundamental changes are needed in the way we conceive and structure our relationships, particularly our heterosexual relationships. These social changes involve changes in the ways men and women view each other and themselves. This issue needs to be addressed by changes in socialization practices—how we raise our children; changes in media images and social constructions of male, female, and sexuality; changes in attitudes, prejudices, and stereotypes about men and women; and changes in behaviors that objectify and violate the Other.

Policy changes and legislation can go only so far in promoting the kind of societal attitude change that will result in respect for women and for women's capacity to share equally in society. Certainly, we can pass laws that prohibit some kinds of behavior: sexual harassment, the use of children in pornography, the airing of violent sexual imagery. But laws cannot by themselves change attitudes or fully eliminate behaviors that reinforce the social structures that oppress women. In fact, efforts to mandate acceptance and equal treatment for specific groups often result in a backlash against those groups. Witness the many forms of the backlash against women we are currently experiencing (Faludi, 1991) or the backlash against affirmative action policies, renamed "preferential treatment." If, however, we could work for a world in which the media images presented of women were primarily positive—showing women of all colors, sexualities, ages, physical appearances, and physical abilities acting competently; showing women in diverse roles, working in partnership with men, and being respected by men for their intelligence, their competency, their efforts—then I believe we would have an impact on how we all think about women.

Many people end up concluding that the efforts for such massive attitudinal change need to be directed at children before they have formed negative images and conceptualizations about women. Psychologists recognize that the socialization resulting in internalized psychic constructs about people and the world begins at birth, with the way primary caretakers relate with and react to the child. Certainly, gender differentiation messages and practices are one of the primary forces operating on a child from the moment of birth. In these early years, before exposure to media images, institutional policies, and extrafamilial and peer influences, it is the primary caretaker(s) whose attitudes, interpretations, and concepts are conveyed to and internalized by the child. This intergenerational learning of sexist attitudes and gender-differentiated roles and behaviors is a difficult process to interrupt, because it is the adult parents or caretakers whose attitudes need to change if a different message is to be passed on to their children.

My point in wandering into the wilderness of attitudinal change, changes in socialization practices, and changes in media images is to convey not only the enormity and the interactive nature of the problem but also the difficulty in deciding at what point to try interceding. It also allows me to be clear about the variety of social actions a counselor could include as part of the counseling activity. Different women will have different interests and skills, which will determine where and how they can most effectively direct their social actions. The point of this counseling model is not to suggest only one type of action appropriate for eradicating violence against women. The point is to help the battered woman not only identify the source of her problem as located in society but also be convinced that any activity directed toward the source—that is, social action—reinforces the understanding that battering is not an individual problem but a social problem. In response to the enormity of the social problem and to the variety of issues that contribute to the denigration of women and battering, we may all be tempted at times to throw up our hands and think, What's the use? But, as radical feminist activists and counselors, we must resist that impulse and work in concert with our battered women clients to intervene in areas they think are important and where they think they can have an impact.

What kinds of social actions can affect popular culture's images of women? We, battered women and counselors, can complain directly to producers of such images: network television, magazines, record companies. We can organize boycotts of products offered for sale by advertisers who support programming and images that degrade, trivialize, and further oppress women. Where the law allows it, we can bring class action lawsuits when we think women have been harmed by such images. We can produce alternative media that promote more positive images of women.

What kinds of social actions can affect socialization practices that continually reproduce a gender-differentiated population in which men hold power over women? We, battered women and counselors, can develop parent training classes that support the values of equality between men and women and give more accurate information about the relatively small sex differences in biology and behavior. We can complain about toys that promote stereotyped images of men and women or encourage violent behavior. We can encourage schools to adopt textbooks that include women and women's contributions to society on a par with men. We can challenge the notion of "family" as being limited to a heterosexual, two-parent household, with two and one half children, and we can expand our definition to include the variety of family alternatives that are practiced in our society (Hite, 1994). We can promote ideals of equality between women and men, particularly in intimate loving relationships.

Outcomes

Of course, the social actions I am suggesting are not new. Feminists have been involved in these kinds of actions for decades. But I am asserting that it is not only appropriate but essential for counselors of battered women to encourage their clients to become engaged in these activities. This style of counseling intervention—one that incorporates social change activities into the work with an individual battered woman —accomplishes both the broader goal of attacking the social roots of battering and two objectives at the individual level.

First, it satisfies one of the needs my research identified by promoting affiliation with women as a group over romantic love with a single partner. Feminists have analyzed how the Western idea of romantic love has often contributed to women's oppression. It is frequently helpful to battered women if they can learn to give up some of their notions of romantic love (cf. Jones, 1994): the idea of one true love in a lifetime, the idea that all of one's needs for connection ought to be satisfied by a single individual, the idea that a woman should put up with any behavior to sustain a relationship. This is not to say that people ought not have committed long-term, sometimes lifelong, intimate relationships. But it is to argue that those relationships ought to be based in equality and mutual caring. If battered women can change their ideas of romantic love, they might be able to find other, nonabusive sources of affiliation. That is, battered women may come to see that part of their need for intimacy, connection, and caring can be met by working with other women on social change to end violence against women. Of course, they begin to attain this sense of affiliation first through the interpersonal relationship with the counselor.

The second objective accomplished by social change activity is that such activity itself is both healing and empowering at the individual level. Taking action to address one's problems heals emotional wounds and develops a sense of self-efficacy and competency. For this reason, most psychologists encourage clients to take action in their individual lives. But in traditional psychotherapeutic frameworks, actions for political change are seldom encouraged. I believe that involvement in social change activities is a crucial step in the development of self-efficacy and competence in battered women. The action encouraged within a social change framework is collective action against a problem larger than the individual situation. It involves not only a sense of empowerment but also the opportunity to practice power strategies. Again, because the root of the individual problem of battering lies in the power relations between women and men that are supported by socialization processes and social institutions, the most effective way for the individual to work on the root of the problem is to work for change in society.

Role of the Subversive Counselor: Social Activist

Just as women's problems demarcate women's needs, and needs define the most effective counseling intervention, the counseling interventions I've suggested as part of this model determine several aspects of the counselor's role. Certainly, parts of the counselor's role, even within this politicized counseling framework, are the traditional humanistic ones of empathic listener, resource provider, companion, and guide; however, the role that becomes the distinguishing feature in subversive counseling is social change activist. It becomes prominent because of the counselor's identifying that the source of an individual battered woman's problem lies in our social and political structures and is maintained by societal attitudes, prejudices, policies, and behaviors. The counselor is convinced that the best way to help the individual battered woman is to work with her on the social source of the problem. The counselor is a radical feminist activist, not just in part of her life or in some aspects of her work, but in all that she does, including and especially in counseling.

Counselor-Client Relationship: Member-Initiate

As a feminist activist, the primary relationship the counselor engages in with the client is that of member-initiate. Conceptualizing the counseling relationship as a relationship between a counselor, working as a member of a social movement to end woman battering in intimate relationships, and a client who is, by coming to counseling, taking her first steps as an initiate in the movement, does not preclude the incorporation of other conceptualizations of the counseling relationship. For example, within battered women's programs, conceptualizing the relationship as a peer, woman to woman, or battered woman to battered woman relationship is often helpful in promoting a shared identification as women working together on a problem. Also, viewing some aspects of the relationship as consultant-seeker or teacher-student is effective in engaging the client in counseling. But just as the counselor's ultimate goal within this model is to identify and work with the client on changing the social conditions that promote battering, so is the featured relationship that of social movement member and initiate.

The client is being offered the opportunity to engage in social change activities that act on the source of her problem, and by doing so, she is being initiated into the battered women's movement. The client can be considered an initiate as she is first exposed to alternative ideas about the role and value of women; as she comes to make the connection between the personal, the political, and taking action to seize power; as she experiences collective participation and decision making in the program; as she becomes involved in the volunteer work of the program; and as she begins to connect—through caucus work and by attending meetings—to the state, national, and international networks and organizations that embody the social movement to end violence against women.

Opportunities for Practicing Power. One of the reasons I distinguish the counselor role from the counselor-client relationship within the structure of this model is to focus more clearly on the analysis of power within the counseling relationship. Recall that this has been a central concern for feminist therapists since the early 1970s. Some have asserted that there ought to be no power discrepancies between counselor and client, that the feminist counseling relationship is a relationship between equals. Others have argued that there are power asymmetries inherent in any counseling relationship, and what the feminist therapist tries to do is make power a point of discussion so that power can be more nearly equalized between counselor and client. Still others point out that there are different types of power and that power can be used in different ways. These theorists argue for sharing power in the counseling relationship, rather than using power over the client.

Whenever two people come together in a relationship of any kind, whether for helping, for friendship, or for love and sexuality, power asymmetries emerge because of the differences between the individuals. Differences can occur on a variety of dimensions: in motivation, in emotional responsiveness, in goals, in roles, in problem-solving capacity, in knowledge about specific topics, in race, sexual orientation, and social class. In good interpersonal relationships, one person doesn't hold all the power, and that is true of good counseling relationships as well. But for counseling, it is essential that the different reasons for initiating the relationship be kept in focus.

The counseling relationship is a special one in which two people come together for a particular purpose. That purpose defines the relationship asymmetrically. That is, one party comes to the relationship seeking assistance with an issue; the other is there to provide assistance, rather than to ensure that her own needs are met. If the assistance provider, the counselor, begins to seek gratification of her own needs from the other party, the client, the counseling contract has been broken. So I situate myself, with regard to this question of power in the counseling relationship, within the tradition of those who work to identify the inevitable power asymmetries in the relationship and attempt to provide opportunities for clients to practice power both in the relationship and in the broader social context in which we live.

As for the power aspects in a counseling relationship between social movement member and initiate, and for the other counseling relationships I have described as included under this rubric, I would acknowledge that there are power asymmetries built into a relationship between two people whose purposes in the relationship are different. That is, one is seeking help; the other is providing help. A counselor, who at the outset views herself as part of a larger feminist movement for social change, presumably has more knowledge about the movement's conceptualizations of the social problem exemplified by the individual battered woman's plight. The initiate, by definition, is learning about the movement's ideology and its application to her situation. The primary strategy of the counselor is to share her knowledge and her power with the battered woman and, at the same time, join with her in seizing power and practicing power opportunities to change the social and political systems that have historically oppressed women.

Together, these components frame a counseling model that is theoretically consistent with a radical feminist ideological model for social change. Within the framework of this model, social change activities are integral to the counseling work with individual battered women. The counselor works with the client to focus on the larger social problem, and in doing so, the individual gains both personal power and collective sociopolitical power.

A Case Study of Subversive Counseling

I first met Kim when I responded to a hotline call from our local hospital. I was the volunteer worker that night for the rape and domestic violence center in our rural county. Kim, 20 years old, had been badly beaten and needed a safe place to stay. She was concerned about her two young sons who were still at home. I accompanied Kim to our battered women's shelter—a small house in a residential setting—and introduced her to another woman staying in the shelter. The three of us talked about possible strategies for getting her sons. Kim decided she would go home in the morning right before her husband left for work, as if she were returning to stay. She would get the children and some things from the house and return to the shelter after her husband went to work.

Kim did not return to the shelter that day. I called her later and asked if it was safe for her to talk. She was very apologetic and told me how remorseful her husband had been when she returned. She was still angry but thought it was important to try to keep the marriage together for the children. I let her know that we—the battered women's program—would be there if and when she needed us again. I helped her think about some plans for her future safety and escape, should she need them.

One of the drawbacks of hotline work is that the volunteer has limited opportunities for follow-up with any particular client. As time went on, I occasionally heard about Kim and her contacts with our program. By the time I became director of the program, 4 years after I first met Kim, I knew that she had completed our volunteer training and was occasionally staffing the hotline. Although she had separated from her abusive husband, she still occasionally suffered from his visits to the children and his continued intimidation and threats toward her. As director, I had somewhat limited contact with our clients. Volunteer training and supervision was the province of our program coordinator; counselors handled the ongoing counseling. I knew that Kim was using our counseling services and was an increasingly active volunteer but, in line with our policy about client confidentiality, I did not pry into the details of her case. As the overall supervisor for the program, however, I knew the kind of counseling, training, and information Kim was encountering through her contact with us. Kim was encountering a radical feminist analysis of the root causes of violence against women and had joined the social movement to end such violence by becoming a volunteer with our program. In counseling, she continued to both analyze her personal connections to women's oppression and practice strategies for seizing power in her own life and in the lives of other battered women.

I left the program after 6 years, having completed my doctorate and obtained a position at our local university. By that time, Kim was enrolled in school, pursuing a degree in psychology. She continued to work with the battered women's program, sometimes as a part-time employee, often as a volunteer. Kim took to dropping by my office, for she was also enrolled in the women's studies concentration that I coordinate. She would talk about her current circumstances as if I were thoroughly familiar with the details of her entire history, sharing her struggles in raising her sons, her conflicts with people and policies in the battered women's program, and her increasing sense of self-worth and self-identity as a feminist counselor. She would talk about the "outrageous" behavior and attitudes of certain professors and discuss different ways to confront and challenge them. In her senior year, she enrolled in the women's studies seminar I co-taught, and I was able to read her papers, which clearly demonstrated a finely tuned feminist analysis and a clear and direct writing style. I began talking with her about graduate school, a possibility she had not considered. As she began taking this idea seriously and saw that it might be possible, she applied to two smaller graduate programs in psychology, which had relatively lower academic standards for acceptance. I urged her to think about a more prestigious and academically rich program that was also in commuting distance. It took some effort to convince her that she and her work might be worthy of such a program, but she eventually asked me to write a letter to this university in support of her application.

Kim graduated from our undergraduate institution last year. She was accepted into the prestigious graduate school, in a social work program, and has started her study there. Kim, I believe, is a classic example of how a battered woman can be helped at the individual level if she is lucky enough to encounter counselors and helpers who are radical, feminist, and activist, willing to enjoin their clients in helping make the world a better place for all women. Clearly, not all battered women will accomplish what Kim will. But when provided the opportunity to understand that their problem is our problem, that their solution lies in eradicating the social roots of our problem, and that their self-worth is enhanced by collective action with other women to change the world, many will accomplish a great deal. Their lives and experiences will touch and inevitably radicalize other women's lives and experiences, because their personal has truly become political. Their experiences of abuse and violence have been transformed into social action.

Carrying It on

As feminists who seek to end male violence against women and other forms of patriarchal domination, we need to connect our vision and theories of radical feminist social change to the praxis of counseling. The subversive model offered here is one means for potentially transforming our helping activities, but the model will remain only a *theoretical* connection unless we are also committed to implementing it in practice. I urge those of you who read this book and are inspired to strive for social change to carry it on by consistently fomenting subversion and the collective action of women and other freedom fighters in your counseling work. To put this theory, this model, into practice, we must urge our professional schools of counseling and our alternative, self-help systems to incorporate the model. We must be able to respond to a conservative backlash that charges us with imposing a political agenda on malleable victims. We must also understand the ways in which this model has broader applicability than the work with battered women.

Professional Training

I have illustrated throughout this text some of the ways in which I believe professionalism, as defined by the battered women's movement, is not the problem. The battered women's movement tends to equate professionalism with education in institutions of higher learning, particularly education that has led to undergraduate and graduate degrees in disciplines such as psychology, counseling, social work, and nursing. Thus, women who are educated, trained, and identified as psychologists, counselors, social workers, or nurses are considered to have professionalist values that hamper identifying with battered women and identifying woman battering as a social rather than an individual problem. The alternative to professionalism, offered by the battered women's movement, is to hold up battered women as the exemplars for providing services to other battered women. In my view, this alternative establishes a false dichotomy between battered women and women who are professionally trained in counseling skills. As I have pointed out before, some professional counselors can be battered women; and some battered women can be professional counselors, receiving their education and training as counselors either prior or subsequent to battering. In fact, the attacks on professionalism tend to discourage battered women from seeking further education. Furthermore, having been battered guarantees neither an understanding of the social roots of woman battering nor the ability to connect in a helping relationship to another battered woman.

It is important to have basic counseling skills when building a relationship with a battered woman who is seeking help. Those skills can be learned in a variety of settings; they include the ability to listen empathically, validate the woman's experience, and respond to the concerns and issues she raises. Typically, they are taught in undergraduate and graduate programs of clinical psychology, counseling, social work, and nursing; however, education and training in institutions of higher education is not the only way to acquire these counseling skills. The volunteer training in battered women's programs that I am familiar with also teaches these skills and gives participants the opportunity to practice them. Regardless of the setting in which these skills are taught and despite our best efforts, some people are more effective than others in employing these skills. Although I agree that basic counseling skills are an essential prerequisite for helping battered women, I am arguing that they are not sufficient. Rather than creating a false dichotomy between professionals (those who have counseling skills) and battered women (those who have experienced the problem of battering), I believe a more fruitful distinction can be made between those counselors who hold a radical feminist understanding of the social roots of battering and those who do not yet have that understanding.

I have become convinced, through working in the battered women's movement and through my research, that the ideological understanding that analyzes the root causes of battering in patriarchal society is what is essential to helping battered women. This analysis must become internalized in counselors who work in battered women's programs until it is so integral to their thinking that their practices automatically reflect the analysis. Moreover, those who work as counselors in battered women's programs must have a counseling model to draw on that incorporates the analysis. They must eventually internalize this model so that they are continually working to understand the battered woman's presenting problems as survival behaviors. They must be convinced that the battered woman's primary need is to engage in social change activities so she can attack the root of her problems in our social and political structures and practices. Counselors must have a thorough understanding of the diverse social determinants of woman battering so that they can help the battered woman identify the areas in which to take action. Counselors must have a variety of potential actions to suggest, to model, and to engage in with the battered woman. Counselors must be convinced that it is social action that promotes both individual empowerment and healing and social changes in the root causes of battering.

The battered women's movement has spent far too much energy and wasted too many years in creating its dichotomy of professionals versus battered women and in attacking professionalism. Instead, I encourage the movement to focus its efforts first on ensuring that its workers are continually trained in the ideological analysis and this counseling model. Those who work in the battered women's movement are truly the professionals in this area, and we should embrace that designation. We who are battered women working in programs and we who, though not battered, work with battered women in shelters are the experts. We know about the societal roots of battering and know what changes need to be made. Rather than insulating ourselves from professional training programs, we ought to be directing a proportion of our efforts toward pressuring educational programs to incorporate our analysis, our models and expertise, so that graduates of such programs, no matter where they practice, will have been exposed to our models.

The Imposition of Values

The belief that counselors ought not impose their values on clients, when carried to the extreme, results in the counselor supporting every decision of the battered woman, no matter how endangering or how deeply it plunges the woman into a situation that continues to degrade and oppress her. Most of us would agree that it is irresponsible to support such decisions without attempting to provide information and options that might deter further abuse. But counselors, at least the counselors in my study, sometimes fail to remember the feminist analysis that no counseling endeavor is free from values. It is neither an appropriate nor a realistic goal to attempt to make counseling value-free. Rather, what we ought to do as counselors is make our values explicit.

One might argue that counselors, even if they agree that they ought to make their values explicit, should still refrain from imposing those values on the client. The underlying assumption in this belief is that it is possible to impose one's values on another, to make her accept those values as her own without even being aware that this is happening. Yet, social psychologists have amply demonstrated how resistant to change firmly held values can be. The purpose in a counselor's making her values explicit is to open those values for discussion and challenge. It is when values operate covertly, and that action is denied, that they influence the counseling activity in unethical ways. The unethical practice is one in which the counselor, without acknowledging or identifying what is happening, manipulates the client into behavior that is commensurate with the counselor's goals and values. Within the counseling model I have proposed, the job of the counselor is to assist the battered woman in identifying the societal sources of her problem. Once these sources are identified, the way to solve the problem includes acting on the source to effect social and political change. Through counseling, the battered woman is joined by the counselor in taking social action. The results of such action include not only societal changes that will cumulatively move us toward our vision but also individual feelings of empowerment, affiliation, and healing that result in more fulfilling lives.

Applications to the Problem of Sexual Violence

I developed this counseling model specifically to work with battered women, but when I initially conceptualized and carried out the case study that started me thinking about the connections between feminist ideology and counseling practice, I was the director of a community-based women's center that responded to the needs of both sexual assault victims and battered women. In addition to my local work in this rural Pennsylvania community, I participated in both the state and the national organizations that supported the work of programs like the one I directed. I considered myself to be part of two feminist movements for social change: the battered women's movement and the anti-rape movement.

Given this context, I want to consider how the counseling model I have described—a model developed to encourage clients to subvert the societal systems of oppression—might apply to work in sexual assault programs with sexual assault victims of all kinds. Because one's ideological understandings inevitably inform one's counseling practice, it is important to begin with an ideological understanding about sexual violence and its roots in society. I am using the phrase *sexual violence* to refer to the entire range of unwanted sexual and sex-related acts that occur between all possible combinations of people. To complicate things a bit further, by *unwanted* I mean not only those acts that are consciously unwanted at the time they occur but also those acts that, though they may be partly desired and consented to at the time, either are unconsciously, ambivalently unwanted or result in effects that are damaging, so that in retrospect the act becomes one that was unwanted by the victim. For example, I will include by this definition an act of date rape in which a female, partly desiring sexual activity but believing it best not to have sex at that moment, gives so-called mixed messages about her desires, beliefs, intentions, and decisions. When forced sex occurs, she might feel a degree of responsibility for what happened, but at the same time might feel that she was raped—that she was forced into unwanted sex. The effects of this rape may be as physically and emotionally damaging as any rape by a stranger. I will include by this definition acts of sexual activity between father and daughter or brother and sister in which the daughter or sister partly desires the sexual contact—because it feels good and brings her some measure of "love" and closeness. Yet, at some point, these activities are likely to be experienced as abusive and exploitative, hence unwanted in retrospect. I will include by this definition so-called consensual sexual relations between a doctor and a patient, a therapist and a client, a teacher and a student. Though such contacts may be consciously wanted when they occur, they may later have damaging effects when the relationship ends or the person with more power moves on to another patient, client, or student. So, these contacts and relationships may also come to be experienced as abusive and exploitative, hence unwanted in retrospect. It is important to consider this entire range of possibilities, because these are some of the experiences people bring to rape centers when seeking counseling. It is also important to encompass the full spectrum of sexual violence, including pornography and prostitution, as well as such acts as leering, ogling, sexual comments, grunts, and catcalls, which are popularly viewed as nonviolent. Although these instances of sexual violence may not be the immediate precipitant for someone's seeking counseling, they are part of the daily experience of almost every woman. In counseling, when such acts get named as acts of sexual violence, they often become both recognized for the intrusive, degrading, and humiliating effects they produce and understood as tools for controlling and dominating women.

In undertaking an ideological analysis of sexual violence in our society, I note the following facts. The vast majority of the entire range of sexually violent acts in our society is perpetrated by adult heterosexual males on females of all races, social classes, ages, and sexualities (Pennsylvania Coalition Against Rape [PCAR], 1990). The second highest incidence of sexual violence is perpetrated by adult heterosexual males on other males—either adult gay males or male children (PCAR, 1990). The other combined categories of perpetrator-victim have a much smaller incidence of sexual violence. Those categories include rape by homosexuals, that is, rape between gay men or between lesbians; child to child sexual violence; adult female to child sexual abuse; and adult female to adult male sexual violence. Because the preponderance of sexual violence is perpetrated by those with power in society against those with less power, it is appropriate to conclude that sexual violence is primarily an act of domination and control. Throughout our society, and specifically in acts of sexual violence, the overwhelming profile is that of men dominating and violating women, gay men, and children. Therefore, acts of sexual violence can be interpreted as perpetuating and reinforcing patriarchal systems of domination. Although this analysis does not preclude the possibility of some individual deviance, that is, psychologically sick persons who are pedophiles or schizophrenic or compulsively acting out their own histories of abuse, it does insist that the larger picture is one in which sexual violence is used as a terroristic tool of domination. Because, by this analysis, the roots of sexual violence lie in patriarchal society, the way to end sexual violence is through social change that transforms the systems of domination and oppression.

So, for me, despite its complexity, the ideological analysis of sexual violence is similar to the ideological analysis of woman battering. In both kinds of violence, the majority of perpetrators are men who commit acts of violence against women, children, and gay men. These acts serve to terrorize and control not only the direct victims but also all women, children, and homosexuals. Such acts benefit both the male perpetrator of violence and men as a group. Because the roots of both sexual violence and woman battering can be seen to lie in society, in patriarchal systems of domination, those systems must be eradicated. If we, as counselors, believe that sexual violence is rooted in society, then the best way to help victims will be to direct their efforts toward social change.

If we adopt the model I have proposed for working with battered women, we can see how it might apply to working with victims of sexual assault. A woman has been raped; a child has been sexually violated by a parent; a gay man has been beaten and sodomized. The problems presented to counselors by clients in these situations include concerns for the physical and emotional consequences or concomitants of the assault. In addition to feeling violated, there are often feelings of terror that such abuse might happen again. In addition to feelings of terror, there may be fantasies or impulses toward revenge. Taken as a whole, the problem presented by sexual assault victims is the fact of sexual violence that has harmed them and has the potential for harming them, or someone they know, again. If the problem is sexual violence in society, then the need of sexual assault victims is to eliminate the roots of that violence. When counselors look at client problems and needs from this perspective, their interventions must be focused on helping the client understand the roots of her or his individual experience of sexual violence and directing the client toward activities that can help transform the social context.

Many of the social change activities that were suggested for battered women can also be useful to victims of sexual violence. First, there are the consciousness-raising practices that connect personal experience to collective understanding to political action. Second, there may be opportunities for clients to participate in the volunteer training of the program and subsequently work with the program. In volunteering to work with the program, clients join the anti-rape movement that seeks to end all sexual violence. They can become connected with state and national organizations that promote social action to eliminate violence and eradicate systems of oppression. Within the movement, they can participate in caucuses that seek political change for specific populations—for example, caucuses for gays or lesbians, for women of color, or for children's rights. Third, there may be opportunities for direct action against perpetrators of sexual violence or against institutions or public officials who are insensitive to the social problem of sexual violence. And finally, there is the experience of radical feminist counseling itself, which offers opportunities for the client within the counseling relationship to challenge power hierarchies and practice power strategies. As in the application of this model to battered women, the result of working with sexual assault victims from this subversive framework is not only the collective growth of the social change movement or the actions that work on the root of the problem in society but also the individual effects of empowerment, self-efficacy, and self-respect.

I have gone through the above analysis of the subversive counseling model as a way of illustrating one of its potential applications. Sexual violence is considered to be primarily a problem experienced by women, though as we have seen, such violence is frequently experienced by children of both sexes and by gay men. So, sexual violence was useful as an illustration in part because it demonstrated that the radical feminist counseling model can work with groups other than women, can be practiced by both male counselors and female, and can be applied to social problems other than so-called women's issues. In fact, I believe that this subversive counseling model can be applied to many other human issues whenever the problem source lies in society and whenever the behavior that results from individual acts of oppression can be construed as behavior in the service of coping, survival, and resistance to further oppression. This is the primary point I am making here. I am not trying to convince all counselors of my ideological understandings of the particular sources of client problems in our society, but I am trying to convince all counselors that they should first consider that society might be the source of the problems experienced by an individual client. When they conclude that society is the source, they should use a counseling approach similar to the one I have described in this book. Let me close by touching upon some of the wide variety of possible circumstances for which my model might be appropriate.

Additional Applications

Another example of the model's potential applicability is for counselors working with gay and lesbian clients. Such clients may come with problems presented as depression, anxiety, or relationship issues. But these problems, like those of battering or sexual violence, can be viewed as problems rooted in society—in this case, the societal oppression of homosexuality. Counselors might ask themselves, if homosexuality were accepted by society as a normal variation in human sexual response, if heterosexuality were not privileged by denying homosexual experience and feelings, if homosexuality were not feared and hated in society, would gay and lesbian clients be experiencing the problems they present? If the problems are rooted in society's heterosexism and homophobia, then the optimum way for gay and lesbian clients to address them is to work on changing the social context.

A similar analysis can be made for other oppressed groups and the problems they present to counselors. Racial, ethnic, and religious groups, other than the white Christian majority in our country, have been historically oppressed and kept in a "one-down" position. At various times in the history of the United States, some immigrant white European groups have been similarly oppressed, like the Irish and the Italians. Jews have been oppressed. Welfare recipients or the homeless can be analyzed as oppressed groups struggling to survive societal, institutional, systemic domination. Working-class peoples, unionized or not, struggle to obtain the resources they need to survive. They are often alienated by their working and living conditions, which could lead them to seek counseling. Middle-class people, in order to achieve the American dream promised by capitalism, seek to accumulate material possessions far beyond what is needed for survival or comfort. Whenever people seek counseling with a sense of alienation, hopelessness, and despair, and we know that the roots of these problems lie in society, counselors and clients together must look to change the social context in which these problems arise. The only hope I see for changing this system of oppression is through social action directed toward societal change. As counselors, we must reexamine the widespread belief within our profession that our job is to help one individual at a time feel better, feel more empowered. In fact, individual feelings of empowerment, in the absence of practicing power, lead to complacency and a reinforcement of the status quo rather than to a transformed society, which is the primary need for many of our clients. So, when counselors find that the sources of their clients' problems are in society, they must direct them toward social change activities that will eventually transform society.

My vision is a world in which all people—women and men, people of color and white, gays and heterosexuals, young and old, able-bodied and disabled—will participate equally in society, join as respectful equals in their personal lives, and share in the responsibilities and rewards of living together. Together, slowly and over time, we will have an impact. I believe my idealized vision is possible to achieve. I see some evidence of this kind of change even today, in a period of vicious backlash against women and progressive reform. I see it in my work setting, at an institution of higher learning, in the way some men relate to women professionally, as colleagues, without introducing sexism and sexuality into the working relationship. I see it in my profession, as the male-dominated American Psychological Association has made some movements, however minor, toward a collegial partnership with women and toward policies that promote change in sexist attitudes and behaviors. I see it in my personal life and in my observations of some intimate relationships in which men and women make commitments to a vision of the sort I describe and then try to live their lives in concert with this vision. Whatever the chances are of achieving the ultimate vision in my lifetime, or in the distant future, I believe it is a vision worth having, a goal worth working toward. To that end, I urge my feminist sisters and my colleagues in psychological and counseling services to consider this subversive model of counseling as one of the tools that can help us work toward that vision. Carry it on.

APPENDIX

Women's Movements in the United States:

Selected Historical Overview From 1963 to the Present

The U.S. Women's Liberation Movement

In 1961, President John Kennedy created the federal Commission on the Status of Women to study the condition of women in the United States. The commission's report was completed by 1963. The recommendations included increased child care services, more opportunities for women in politics, and equal opportunity in employment. The year 1963 also saw the publication of Betty Friedan's *The Feminine Mystique,* a book revealing the post-World War II cultural propaganda that promoted women's "ideal" nature and role as homemaker and mother. Although Friedan stopped short of identifying women as oppressed, her unveiling of the discrepancy between the blissful ideal of the American housewife and the reported unhappiness of (middle-class) women promoted one of the early second wave analyses of the condition of women, by women.

Friedan was also active in forming the National Organization for Women (NOW) in 1966. NOW was created, in keeping with the aims of liberal feminists, to demand equality for women through the existing political system. The original demands of NOW included an equal rights amendment, equal opportunities for education and employment, maternity and child care protections, and reproductive freedom. The liberal feminist vision was that women needed to access their

143

legitimate rights as human beings participating in a democratic state. Many political groups with goals promoting women's interests were formed in this decade, including the Women's Equity Action League (1969) and the National Women's Political Caucus (1971). Women involved in these groups were convinced that this effort to include women in the traditional structures of liberal democratic society was essential. These women were not fundamentally challenging the nature of the state.

In the latter part of the 1960s, however, a growing number of women in New Left organizations began to raise more fundamental questions. Sara Evans (1979) points out that these questions were first raised by both black and white women working in the civil rights movement. Women's developing sense of personal strength and self-respect was discovered within an ideology of equality between whites and blacks as civil rights workers; however, this fundamental belief in equality, coupled with the contradictory treatment women were receiving as women, eventually led to the emergence of a social movement specifically for women's liberation.

Evans (1979) explores the interconnections between the later civil rights movement and the student New Left. As black activists began to examine the economic and power disparities between blacks and whites in the United States, many of the younger new leaders found that Marxism offered an analysis that seemed relevant to the conditions they were confronting in America. In effect, this younger, more radical wing of the civil rights movement broke with the traditions of those represented by Martin Luther King, Jr. Although King had basically argued for the inclusion of black Americans in the existing political system, black nationalists, like the student New Left, began questioning the system itself. As black nationalism grew, white activists were increasingly excluded from participation in this effort, and groups like Students for a Democratic Society (SDS) became the available organizations for whites desiring to join the movement. Many white women, who had begun to achieve a sense of identity and a commitment to social justice in the civil rights movement, now continued their efforts with groups like SDS.

Most historians, however, ignore the important role of women's experiences in the early civil rights movement and simply assert that the primary impetus for second wave feminism came from leftist women's growing dissatisfaction with their role and treatment in the New Left (Freeman, 1995). The radical New Left in the 1960s was active in criticizing not only American capitalist society but also the old Left's support of bureaucratic and totalitarian Soviet Russia. New Left student activism initially took the form of joining the civil rights movement (e.g., Freedom Summer in 1964). But later, students began agitating for the civil rights of students (e.g., the Free Speech Movement), then moved on to organize against the Vietnam war. Despite the purported equality within these leftist groups, women found themselves denied leadership, their voices silenced by males and their roles reduced to coffee maker and sexual companion. New Left women began talking among themselves, giving voice to their concerns as women and, more important, organizing for change.

A 1966 publication by Juliet Mitchell, "Women: The Longest Revolution," offered a Marxist analysis of women as a class. Mitchell contended that there were four structures, common to women, in need of transformation: production, reproduction, socialization, and sexuality. This article was widely circulated among radical women in New Left groups like SDS and promoted thinking about women as a group across economic classes (Echols, 1989). In 1967, SDS approved a women's manifesto, which had been developed in a workshop on women's liberation.

Subsequent to the SDS women's manifesto, groups for women's liberation began to sprout all over the United States. For example, Women's Radical Action Project formed in Chicago; in New York it was New York Radical Women. These groups and others like them chose the term *radical* to emphasize their alliance with New Left politics. Radical was initially chosen by women's liberationists because the ultimate goal was to eliminate the current political system and replace it with a new system—one that would value women, include women's perspectives, create incentives for women and men to participate equally in all spheres (private and public), and free women from the male violence that was used as a method of controlling women in the current system. Radical means "root," and radical feminists hoped to get to the root of women's oppression and eradicate it from the new society they hoped to build. This ideology distinguished these feminists from the liberal feminists who had fought to win women various rights within the existing political system. Because of their experience in the New Left, where organizational structure and process continued to oppress women despite the stated goals of equality and classlessness, these groups stressed the importance of keeping the structure and process of their groups aligned with their long-term goal of liberating women. They therefore sought to abolish traditional hierarchical and bureaucratic structures and promoted the techniques of consciousness-raising, leaderless groups, consensus decision making, and shared responsibility. Although similar themes had also emerged in the civil rights and New Left movements, the lack of a sex-class analysis of oppression usually excluded women from these equality efforts.

As women's liberation groups began to multiply, new groups often developed out of ideological disagreements or refinements around a particular issue. For instance, Redstockings, which formed in early 1969, emphasized an analysis that the oppression of the sex-class system was the primary oppression. They insisted that other oppressions, such as classism and racism, developed historically later. New York Radical Feminists formed when organizers felt that Redstockings was focusing on consciousness-raising to the relative exclusion of direct action. Meanwhile Ti-Grace Atkinson, a protege of Betty Friedan in the National Organization for Women, had started a group called the Feminists to protest against NOW's lack of commitment to eliminating hierarchy and sharing power among women. The Feminists started many leaderless groups in New York, arguing that they were working to annihilate the sex-role system (Atkinson, 1974). Some groups argued that (heterosexual) women need to stop collaborating with the male system of oppression and should refuse sexual relationships with men. Other groups became the focal point for specific lesbian feminist theorizing.

By 1970, the women's liberation movement was a hot item for news coverage in the United States. Unfortunately for women's liberation, the popular media failed to recognize the subtle ideological distinctions being articulated by various groups and chose instead to focus on the divisiveness among feminists. Certainly, there was ideological disagreement among feminist groups, but its roots were varied. By 1970, the women's liberation movement was being challenged from within by groups of women with particular concerns, including radical lesbians, women of color, working-class women, and older women, calling attention to their particular needs and their multiple oppressions.

The Battered Women's Movement

Historically, the battered women's movement, or the shelter movement, is typically spoken of as having moved to the United States from Great Britain (Martin, 1976). Part of the reason for this interpretation is that London may have been the site of the first battered women's shelter. A Women's Aid Center was opened in London in 1971 to respond generally to concerns of women. The center quickly became inundated with calls from abused women and began taking in these women to provide them temporary shelter. Erin Pizzey (1974) documents some of the work of that center in one of the first books published about woman battering.

According to Susan Schechter's comprehensive history and analysis (1982), the battered women's movement in the United States developed as a visible force about 4 years after the British movement. Still, one of the first hotlines established in the United States appeared at Women's Advocates in St. Paul, Minnesota, around 1972, just shortly after the first British center; by 1974, they had an established shelter for battered women. In 1976, the first U.S. books about abuse were published, analyzing *domestic violence* or *wifebeating* as based in beliefs about sex roles and the institutional arrangements that result from these beliefs, especially marriage and the traditional family. Specifically, woman battering was seen as a means of controlling women and keeping them in their proper role.

Women (and men) are socialized to believe that the ultimate life goal is marriage, that the woman's role is to serve her husband, that the man is king of his castle, and that his word is law within the home.

Radical and socialist feminists organized the first battered women's shelters in the United States. Many of these shelters evolved out of the work of more general women's centers established in the early 1970s. It appears that battered women's need for help was so great that many centers decided to make this work their full-time function, so around 1975, the first identifiable battered women's shelters and programs emerged. By 1978, more than 300 shelters were established nationally (Deckard, 1979); now, in the mid-1990s, there are close to 1,500 shelters and programs (NCADV, 1994).

In an effort to acknowledge and praise the diversity of women comprised in the battered women's movement, Schechter (1982) provides an analysis of the unique contributions of various groups of feminist women to the movement. For example, Third World feminists helped the movement understand the double oppressions of race and sex, and lesbian feminists added an analysis of the oppression of heterosexism and homophobia and contributed a commitment to the form of women working with women. Moreover, the analysis of radical feminists, which argues that the organization of the home and family creates a climate for woman battering, led to the alternative system approach to working with battered women, resulting in autonomous women's programs and collective work models based in consensus decision making. Furthermore, it was socialist feminists who promoted the understanding that battered women are fighting not only the oppression of patriarchy but also that of class and race. This understanding led to an acknowledgment that at times men and women can have interests in common as workers, as members of the same race, or as family members. Moreover, it led to an acknowledgment that there are differences among women that sometimes supersede their commonalities as women.

The National Coalition

Although the diversity of perspectives offered by these different groups of women has created a climate that has the potential for mutual understanding, it has often led to conflicts among women committed to helping battered women. The history of the National Coalition Against Domestic Violence (NCADV) illustrates some of the benefits and difficulties of attempting to incorporate sometimes diametrically opposed views. NCADV was formed in 1978, during a U.S. Commission on Civil Rights consultation on battered women; however, planning for such a group had started more than a year and a half earlier, at a 1976 conference on battered women in Wisconsin. The following year, at the 1977

International Women's Year conference in Houston, a caucus of grassroots bat-tered women's programs passed a battered women's resolution for presentation to President Carter. These networking opportunities had established the basis for the formation of NCADV in 1978 (Bako, 1979).

NCADV's first effort was to encourage passage of federal legislation authoriz-ing funds for services to battered women. Many feminists expressed concerns about the potential co-optative effects of accepting government funding. The question of funding is an example of how, from the beginning, NCADV's complex coalition of women from widely diverse areas of the United States had difficulties coming to consensus on a number of important questions, including the question of whether to be outspokenly radical and feminist. For example, Johnson (1981) and Morgan (1981) point out that accepting money from the government could have the effect of limiting radical efforts to change society, because the govern-ment represents the society that needs to be changed. The recent establishment by the Clinton administration of an office in the Justice Department to focus on violence against women raises similar concerns. Issues like these epitomize the difficulties often encountered when radical groups attempt to put theory into practice. The coalition has swung both ways over the past 17 years and has managed to achieve a kind of balance that usually manages to keep both radical feminists and liberal reformists involved, though often in extreme conflict with one another.

The Pennsylvania Coalition

A similar type of balancing can be found in PCADV, the Pennsylvania coalition of battered women's programs. PCADV has been viewed as a model program for a state coalition by Schechter (1982) and others (cf. Leghorn, 1982). As such, it has contributed substantially to the ideology of NCADV and the battered women's movement. Pennsylvania is useful as an illustration of the development of the battered women's movement on the statewide level because of its extended history, its organizational structure, its radical purpose, and its stability as a funded group. In Pennsylvania as elsewhere, community women's centers became the source of many battered women's programs. As early as 1973, a shelter was opened by the Women's Center and Shelter of Greater Pittsburgh. By 1975, shelters for battered women had also been opened in Philadelphia, Erie, and Bloomsburg (central Pennsylvania). Hotlines for domestic violence were operating in Delaware and Montgomery counties (suburban Philadelphia) and in Dauphin, Lancaster, and York counties (south central Pennsylvania). Less structured volunteer help groups were scattered in seven other counties (PCADV, 1989). At this stage, most of these groups were operated almost completely by volunteers who had little knowledge of one another's existence.

In 1976, with support from Pennsylvania Legal Services, a Protection from Abuse (PFA) bill was introduced into the Pennsylvania state legislature. The bill was considered model legislation, only the second of its kind in the United States. It provided for a civil means of protecting women from further abuse by a spouse or living partner. A woman would be able to quickly petition the court to have her abuser removed from the home for up to 1 year and have him ordered to pay support for her children. If the court order was violated, the abuser faced immediate arrest on contempt charges.

Nine women from various parts of Pennsylvania, all strangers to each other, met in Harrisburg, in spring 1976, to testify in support of the PFA legislation. They were so excited to discover that there were other groups working with the same problems that they determined to meet again as a group to share information and provide mutual support (PCADV, 1986). These women, along with representatives from other Pennsylvania counties, met next in fall 1976, after the passage of the PFA act. They decided to formally incorporate as the Pennsylvania Coalition Against Domestic Violence. Seventeen programs were represented on the first board of directors. They continued to meet one weekend each month, traveling at their own expense to various parts of the state and staying in one another's homes.

Together, these women organized efforts to contact and lobby legislators, the police, and courts responsible for implementing the PFA act, and state institutions, such as the Department of Public Welfare, whose decisions and policies affected battered women's lives. In 1980, federal Title XX funds—the social services block grants to states—became available. This coalition of women, who had made the needs of battered women so well-known to people in Pennsylvania's government, was approached by the state Department of Public Welfare to manage the contract of funds that had been set aside for domestic violence programs. Since that time, the coalition has grown from its original 17 members to 64 programs, serving all of Pennsylvania's 67 counties.

References

Agel, J. (Ed.). (1971). *The radical therapist.* New York: Ballantine.
Association for Women in Psychology. (1991, March). About AWP: Herstory. In *Women in the 90s: United in diversity.* Conference program from annual AWP conference, Hartford, CT.
Atkinson, T. (1974). *Amazon odyssey.* New York: Link.
Bailey, R., & Brake, M. (Eds.). (1975). *Radical social work.* New York: Pantheon.
Bako, Y. (1979). *Chronological history of the national coalition against domestic violence.* Photocopied notes compiled by a member of the New York Steering Committee representative to NCADV (in author's possession).
Battered/Formerly Battered Women's Task Force. (1992). *A current analysis of the battered women's movement.* Denver: NCADV.
Belenky, M., Clinchy, B., Goldberger, N., & Tarule, J. (1986). *Women's ways of knowing.* New York: Basic Books.
Blechman, E. (1980). Behavior therapies. In A. Brodsky & R. Hare-Mustin (Eds.), *Women and psychotherapy: An assessment of research and practice* (pp. 217-244). New York: Guilford.
Brodsky, A. (1973). The consciousness-raising group as a model for therapy with women. *Psychotherapy: Theory, Research, and Practice, 10,* 24-29.
Brown, L. S. (1994). *Subversive dialogues.* New York: Basic Books.
Brownmiller, S. (1975). *Against our will: Men, women and rape.* New York: Bantam.
Bunch, C. (1972). Lesbians in revolt. *The Furies, 1,* 29-37.
Burris, B. (1973). The fourth world manifesto. In A. Koedt, E. Levine, & A. Rapone (Eds.), *Radical feminism* (pp. 322-357). New York: Quadrangle.

Burstow, B. (1992). *Radical feminist therapy.* Newbury Park, CA: Sage.

Burt, M., Gornick, J., & Pittman, K. (1984). *Feminism and rape crisis centers.* Washington, DC: Urban Institute.

Butler, S. (1985). Guidelines for feminist therapy. In L. Rosewater & L. Walker (Eds.), *Handbook of feminist therapy: Women's issues in psychotherapy* (pp. 32-38). New York: Springer.

Chaplin, J. (1988). *Feminist counseling in action.* London: Sage.

Chesler, P. (1972). *Women and madness.* Garden City, NY: Doubleday.

Chodorow, N. (1978). *The reproduction of mothering: Psychoanalysis and the sociology of gender.* Berkeley: University of California Press.

Combahee River Collective (1977). *The Combahee river collective statement.* New York: Kitchen Table: Women of Color Press.

Cooper, D. (1967). *Psychiatry and anti-psychiatry.* London: Tavistock.

Cronan, S. (1973). Marriage. In A. Koedt, E. Levine, & A. Rapone (Eds.), *Radical feminism* (pp. 213-221). New York: Quadrangle.

Daly, M. (1973). *Beyond god the father: Toward a philosophy of women's liberation.* Boston: Beacon.

Daly, M. (1978). *Gyn-ecology: The metaethics of radical feminism.* Boston: Beacon.

Davis, A. (1981). *Women, race, and class.* New York: Vintage.

Deckard, B. (1979). *The women's movement.* New York: Harper & Row.

Dinnerstein, D. (1976). *The mermaid and the minotaur.* New York: Harper Colophon.

Douglas, M. A. (1985). The role of power in feminist therapy: A reformulation. In L. Rosewater & L. Walker (Eds.), *Handbook of feminist therapy: Women's issues in psychotherapy* pp. 241-249. New York: Springer.

Dutton, D., & Painter, S. (1981). The development of emotional attachments in battered women and other relationships of intermittent abuse. *Victimology, 6,* 139-155.

Dutton, M. A. (1992). *Empowering and healing the battered woman: A model for assessment and intervention.* New York: Springer.

Echols, A. (1989). *Daring to be bad: Radical feminism in America 1967-1975.* Minneapolis: University of Minnesota Press.

Eichenbaum, L., & Orbach, S. (1983). *Understanding women: A feminist psychoanalytic approach.* New York: Basic Books.

Ellis, E. M., & Nichols, M. P. (1979). A comparative study of feminist and traditional group assertiveness training with women. *Psychotherapy: Theory, Research, and Practice, 4,* 467-474.

Evans, S. (1979). *Personal politics: The roots of women's liberation in the civil rights movement and the new left.* New York: Knopf.

Faludi, S. (1991). *Backlash: The undeclared war against American women.* New York: Crown.

Faunce, P. S. (1985a). A feminist philosophy of treatment. In L. Rosewater & L. Walker (Eds.), *Handbook of feminist therapy: Women's issues in psychotherapy* (pp. 1-4). New York: Springer.

Faunce, P. S. (1985b). Teaching feminist therapies: Integrating feminist therapy, pedagogy, and scholarship. In L. Rosewater & L. Walker (Eds.), *Handbook of feminist therapy: Women's issues in psychotherapy* (pp. 309-320). New York: Springer.

Fields, N., & Conrey, D. (1994, July 29-August 3). Classism and empowerment: Have they joined us or have we joined them? In NCADV (Ed.), *Many voices, one vision* (Program for sixth national NCADV conference, St. Paul, MN). Denver: NCADV.

Fine, M. (1985). Unearthing contradictions: An essay inspired by *Women and male violence*. *Feminist Studies, 11*, 391-401.

Fine, M., & Gordon, S. (1991). Effacing the center and the margins: Life at the intersection of psychology and feminism. *Feminism & Psychology, 1*, 19-28.

Firestone, S. (1970). *The dialectic of sex: The case for feminist revolution*. New York: Bantam.

Fodor, I. (1985). Assertiveness training for the eighties: Moving beyond the personal. In L. Rosewater & L. Walker (Eds.), *Handbook of feminist therapy: Women's issues in psychotherapy* (pp. 257-265). New York: Springer.

Freechild, S. (1989, July). *New age healing or age old oppression*. Workshop presented at NCADV conference, Philadelphia.

Freeman, J. (Ed.). (1995). *Women: A feminist perspective* (5th ed.). Mountain View, CA: Mayfield.

Freeman, J. (1972). The tyranny of structurelessness. *Berkeley Journal of Sociology, 17*, 151-164.

Freire, P. (1970). *Pedagogy of the oppressed*. New York: Seabury.

French, J. R. P., Jr., & Raven, B. (1959). The bases of social power. In D. Cartwright (Ed.), *Studies in social power*. Ann Arbor, MI: Institute for Social Research.

Galper, J. (1980). *Social work practice: A radical perspective*. Englewood Cliffs, NJ: Prentice Hall.

Gannon, L. (1982). The role of power in psychotherapy. *Women and Therapy, 1*, 3-11.

Gilbert, L. A. (1980). Feminist therapy. In A. Brodsky & R. Hare-Mustin (Eds.), *Women and psychotherapy* (pp. 245-265). New York: Guilford.

Gilligan, C. (1982). *In a different voice*. Cambridge, MA: Harvard University Press.

Glaser, B., & Strauss, A. (1967). *The discovery of grounded theory: Strategies for qualitative research*. New York: Aldine.

Gondolf, E. (1988). *Battered women as survivors*. Lexington, MA: Lexington Books.

Gore, J. (1992). What we can do for you! What can "we" do for "you"?: Struggling over empowerment in critical pedagogy. In C. Luke & J. Gore (Eds.), *Feminisms and critical pedagogy* (pp. 54-73). New York: Routledge.

Gornick, J., Burt, M., & Pittman, K. (1983). *Structure and activities of rape crisis centers in the early 1980s*. Washington, DC: Urban Institute.

Graham, D., Rawlings, E., & Rimini, N. (1988). Survivors of terror: Battered women, hostages, and the Stockholm syndrome. In K. Ylló & M. Bograd (Eds.), *Feminist perspectives on wife abuse* (pp. 217-233). Beverly Hills, CA: Sage.

Greenspan, M. (1983). *A new approach to women and therapy*. New York: McGraw-Hill.

Griffin, S. (1980). *Woman and nature: The roaring inside her*. New York: Harper & Row.

Halleck, S. (1971). *The politics of therapy*. New York: Harper & Row.

Hanisch, C. (1970). The personal is political. In S. Firestone & A. Koedt (Eds.), *Notes from the second year: Women's liberation*. New York: New York Radical Feminists.

Herman, J. (1992). *Trauma and recovery*. New York: Basic Books.

Hite, S. (1994). *The Hite report on the family: Growing up under patriarchy*. New York: Grove.

Holroyd, J. (1976). Psychotherapy and women's liberation. *Counseling Psychologist, 6*, 22-28.

hooks, b. (1981). *Ain't I a woman?: Black women and feminism*. Boston: South End Press.

Hutchinson, M., & Sandler, H. (1975). *Social change counseling: A radical approach*. Boston: Houghton Mifflin.

Ivey, A. (1976). Counseling psychology, the psychoeducator model and the future. *Counseling Psychologist, 6,* 72-76.

Jacobs, G. (1994). Where do we go from here? An interview with Ann Jones. *Ms., 5,* pp. 56-63.

Jaggar, A. (1983). *Feminist politics and human nature.* Totowa, NJ: Rowman & Allenheld.

Johnson, J. (1981). Program enterprise and official cooperation in the battered women's shelter movement. *American Behavioral Scientist, 24,* 827-842.

Johnson, M. (1976). An approach to feminist therapy. *Psychotherapy: Theory, Research, and Practice, 13,* 72-76.

Jones, A. (1994). *Next time she'll be dead: Battery and how to stop it.* Boston: Beacon.

Kaschak, E. (1981). Feminist psychotherapy: The first decade. In S. Cox (Ed.), *Female psychology* (2nd ed., pp. 387-401). New York: St. Martin's.

Kelly, L. (1986). National coalition against domestic violence conference. *off our backs, 16*(10), 1-5.

Kirsh, B. (1974). Consciousness-raising groups as therapy for women. In V. Franks & V. Burtle (Eds.), *Women in therapy* (pp. 326-354). New York: Bruner/Mazel.

Koedt, A. (1970). Politics of the ego: A manifesto for New York radical feminists. In S. Firestone & A. Koedt (Eds.), *Notes from the second year: Women's liberation* (p. 126). New York: New York Radical Feminists.

Laidlaw, T., & Malmo, C. (1990). *Healing voices: Feminist approaches to therapy with women.* San Francisco: Jossey-Bass.

Laing, R. D. (1967). *The politics of experience.* New York: Ballantine.

Lear, M. (1968, March 10). The second feminist wave. *New York Times Magazine,* pp. 24, 50, 53, 55, 58, 60, 62.

Leghorn, L. (1982). Interview with Susan Schechter. In S. Schechter, *Women and male violence.* Boston: South End Press.

Lerman, H. (1976). What happens in feminist therapy? In S. Cox (Ed.), *Female psychology: The emerging self.* Chicago: Science Research Associates.

Lerman, H. (1985). Some barriers to the development of a feminist theory of personality. In L. Rosewater & L. Walker (Eds.), *Handbook of feminist therapy: Women's issues in psychotherapy* (pp. 5-12). New York: Springer.

Lincoln, Y., & Guba, E. (1985). *Naturalistic inquiry.* Newbury Park, CA: Sage.

Lindsey, K. (1974). On the need to develop a feminist therapy. *Rough Times: A Journal of Radical Therapy, 4,* 2-3.

Lobel, K. (Ed.). (1986). *Naming the violence: Speaking out about lesbian battering.* Seattle: Seal.

Lorde, A. (1984). *Sister outsider.* Trumansberg, NY: The Crossing Press.

Mandel, J. (1994). *How political is the personal: Identity politics, feminism, and social change* (Draft). Copy sent by e-mail, courtesy of J. Mandel, Director of Women's Studies, Colgate University.

Mander, A. V., & Rush, A. K. (1974). *Feminism as therapy.* New York: Random House.

Martin, D. (1976). *Battered wives.* San Francisco: Glide.

Maslow, A. (1954). *Motivation and personality.* New York: Harper.

Maslow, A. (1971). *The farther reaches of human nature.* New York: Viking.

McNees, P. (1994, July 29-August 3). Discriminatory policies regarding battered/formerly battered women working in domestic violence programs. In NCADV (Ed.), *Many voices, one vision* (Program for sixth national NCADV conference, St. Paul, MN). Denver: NCADV.

Miller, J. B. (1976). *Toward a new psychology of women.* Boston: Beacon.

Mitchell, J. (1966, November-December). Women: The longest revolution. *New Left Review,*(40), 17-20.

Mitchell, J. (1974). *Psychoanalysis and feminism.* New York: Pantheon.

Moraga, C. (1981). Preface. In C. Moraga & G. Anzaldua (Eds.), *This bridge called my back: Writings by radical women of color* (pp. xiii-xix). Watertown, MA: Persephone.

Moraga, C., & Anzaldua, G. (Eds.). (1983). *This bridge called my back: Writings by radical women of color.* Watertown, MA: Persephone.

Morgan, P. (1981). From battered wife to program client. The state's shaping of social problems. *Kapitalistate, 9,* 17-39.

Morgan, R. (1975). Interview with Robin Morgan and Adrienne Rich. In K. Grimstad & S. Rennie (Eds.), *The new woman's survival sourcebook* (pp. 106-111). New York: Knopf.

National Coalition Against Domestic Violence. (1994, July 29-August 3). *Many voices, one vision* (Program for sixth national NCADV conference, St. Paul, MN). Denver: Author.

NiCarthy, G. (1984). *Talking it out: A guide to groups for abused women.* Seattle: Seal.

NiCarthy, G. (1988, November). NCADV meets. *off our backs,* 2.

Ochberg, E. (1988). *Post-traumatic therapy and victims of violence.* New York: Bruner/ Mazel.

Pence, E. (1987). *In our best interest: A process for personal and social change.* Duluth: Minnesota Program Development, Inc.

Pence, E., & Shepard, M. (1988). Integrating feminist theory and practice: The challenge of the battered women's movement. In K. Yllo & M. Bograd (Eds.), *Feminist perspectives on wife abuse* (pp. 282-298). Newbury Park, CA: Sage.

Pennsylvania Coalition Against Domestic Violence. (1976a). *Bylaws.* Harrisburg, PA: Author.

Pennsylvania Coalition Against Domestic Violence. (1976b). *Principles of unity.* Harrisburg, PA: Author.

Pennsylvania Coalition Against Domestic Violence. (1986, November). Roundtable discussion on the history of PCADV: Remembrances from the original participants. Author's notes from PCADV's 10th anniversary celebration, Harrisburg, PA.

Pennsylvania Coalition Against Domestic Violence. (1987). *PCADV feminist empowerment model.* Harrisburg, PA: Author.

Pennsylvania Coalition Against Domestic Violence. (1989). *Training Manual.* Harrisburg, PA: Author.

Pennsylvania Coalition Against Rape (PCAR). (1990). *Sexual assault services in Pennsylvania: Making a difference, changing lives.* Harrisburg, PA: Author.

Perkins, R. (1991). Therapy for lesbians?: The case against. *Feminism & Psychology, 1,* 325-338.

Pharr, S. (1988). *Homophobia: A weapon of sexism.* Inverness, CA: Chardon.

Pharr, S. (1989, Summer). Lesbian battering: Social change urged. *NCADV Voice,* 16-17.

Pizzey, E. (1974). *Scream quietly or the neighbors will hear you.* London: Penguin.

Prilleltensky, I. (1994). *The morals and politics of psychology: Psychological discourse and the status quo.* Albany: State University of New York Press.

Prozan, C. (1992). *Feminist psychoanalytic psychotherapy.* Northvale, NJ: Jason Aronson.

Radicalesbians. (1971). The woman-identified woman. In A. Koedt, A. Rapone, & E. Levine (Eds.), *Notes from the third year: Women's liberation* (pp. 240-245). New York: New York Radical Feminists.

Rawlings, E. I., & Carter, D. K. (Eds.). (1977). *Psychotherapy for women: Treatment towards equality.* Springfield, IL: Charles C Thomas.

Rein, M. (1970). *Social policy: Issues of choice and change.* New York: Random House.

Rich, A. (1980). Compulsory heterosexuality and lesbian existence. *Signs, 5,* 648-649.

Richardson, M. S., & Johnson, M. (1984). Counseling women. In S. Brown & R. Lent (Eds.), *Handbook of counseling psychology* (pp. 832-877). New York: John Wiley.

Rigby-Weinberg, D. (1986). A future direction for radical feminist therapy. In D. Howard (Ed.), *A guide to dynamics of feminist therapy* (pp. 191-205). New York: Harrington Park.

Riger, S. (1994). Challenges of success: Stages of growth in feminist organizations. *Feminist studies, 20*(2), 275-300.

Rogers, C. (1961). *On becoming a person: A therapist's view of psychotherapy.* Boston: Houghton Mifflin.

Rohrbaugh, J. B. (1979). *Women: Psychology's puzzle.* New York: Basic Books.

Rose, S. (1972). *Betrayal of the poor: Transformation of community action.* Cambridge, MA: Schenkman.

Ruddick, S. (1980). Maternal thinking. *Feminist Studies, 6,* 342-367.

Ruddick, S. (1983). Preservative love and military destruction: Some reflections on mother and peace. In J. Treblicot (Ed.), *Mothering: Essays in Feminist Theory* (pp. 231-262). Totowa, NJ: Rowman & Allanheld.

Sampson, E. E. (1977). Psychology and the American ideal. *Journal of Personality and Social Psychology, 35,* 767-82.

Sampson, E. E. (1978). Scientific paradigms and social values: Wanted—a scientific revolution. *Journal of Personality and Social Psychology, 36,* 1332-43.

Sampson, E. E. (1981). Cognitive psychology as ideology. *American Psychologist, 36,* 730-43.

Schechter, S. (1982). *Women and male violence: The visions and struggles of the battered women's movement.* Boston: South End Press.

Schechter, S. (1988, June). *Professionalism in the battered women's movement.* Panel conducted at the PCADV annual meeting, Harrisburg, PA.

Scribner, S. (1968). What is community pychology made of? *Newsletter, 11,* American Psychological Association, Division of Community Psychology, 1.

Seligman, M. (1975). *Helplessness: On depression, development and death.* New York: John Wiley.

Sipe, R. (1982). Radical therapy and psychopolitics. *Issues in Radical Therapy, 10,* 12-16.

Smith, A., & Siegel, R. (1985). Feminist therapy: Redefining power for the powerless. In L. Rosewater & L. Walker (Eds.), *Handbook of feminist therapy: Women's issues in psychotherapy* (pp. 13-21). New York: Springer.

Smith, B. (Ed.). (1985). *Home girls: A black feminist anthology.* New York: Kitchen Table: Women of Color Press.

Squire, C. (1989). *Significant differences: Feminism in psychology.* London: Routledge.

Stanley, L., & Wise, S. (1983). *Breaking out: Feminist consciousness and feminist research.* London: Routledge & Kegan Paul.

Steiner, C. (1975). *Readings in radical psychiatry.* New York: Grove.

Stewart, A., & Ostrove, J. (1993). Social class, social change, and gender. *Psychology of Women Quarterly, 17,* 475-497.

Sturdivant, S. (1980). *Therapy with women: A feminist philosophy of treatment.* New York: Springer.

Szasz, T. (1970). *Ideology and insanity.* Garden City, NY: Doubleday.

Thomas, S. (1977). Theory and practice in feminist therapy. *Social Work, 22,* 447-454.

Unger, R. K. (1988). Psychological feminist, and personal epistemology: Transcending contradiction. In M. Gergen (Ed.), *Feminist thought and the structure of knowledge* (pp. 124-141). New York: New York University Press.

Unger, R. K. (1990). Imperfect reflections of reality: Psychology and the construction of gender. In R. Hare-Mustin & J. Marecek (Eds.), *Making a difference: Representations of gender in psychology* (pp. 102-149). New Haven: Yale University Press.

U.S. Department of Justice. (1986). *Special report: Preventing domestic violence against women* (NCJ-102037). Washington, DC: Bureau of Justice Statistics.

Walker, L. (1977). Battered women and learned helplessness. *Victimology, 2,* 535-544.

Walker, L. (1979). *The battered woman.* New York: Harper & Row.

Walker, L. (1980). Battered women. In A. Brodsky & R. Hare-Mustin (Eds.), *Women and psychotherapy: An assessment of research and practice* (pp. 339-363). New York: Guilford.

Walker, L. (1984a). *The battered woman syndrome.* New York: Springer.

Walker, L. (Ed.). (1984b). *Women and mental health policy.* Beverly Hills, CA: Sage.

Walker, L. (1989a). Psychology and violence against women. *American Psychologist, 44,* 695-702.

Walker, L. (1989b). *Terrifying love: Why battered women kill and how society responds.* New York: Harper & Row.

Walker, L. (1994). *Abused women and survivor therapy: A practical guide for the psychotherapist.* Washington, DC: American Psychological Association.

Warrior, B. (1976). *Wifebeating.* Somerville, MA: New England Free Press.

Warrior, B. (1985). *Battered women's directory.* Richmond, IN: Earlham College Press.

Weisstein, N. (1971). Psychology constructs the female. *Journal of Social Education, 35,* 362-73.

Whalen, M. (1988, June). *Professionalism in the battered women's movement.* Panel conducted at the PCADV annual meeting, Harrisburg, PA.

Whalen, M. (1992). *Counseling as a subversive activity: Counseling models in battered women's and anti-rape programs.* Ann Arbor: UMI Dissertation Services.

Williams, B. (1978). The retreat to cultural feminism. In Redstockings (Eds.), *Feminist revolution* (pp. 79-83). New York: Random House.

Willis, E. (1984). Radical feminism and feminist radicalism. In S. Sayres, A. Stephanson, S. Aronowitz, & F. Jameson (Eds.), *The '60's without apology.* Minneapolis: University of Minnesota Press.

Wyckoff, H. (1975). Banal scripts of women. In C. Steiner (Ed.), *Scripts people live: Transactional analysis of life scripts,* pp. 210-234. New York: Bantam.

Author Index

Subject Index

Abuse:
    alcohol and drug, 81
    psychological, 18
    See also Domestic violence
Academic feminists, 25
Activism, social:
    consciousness-raising as, 30, 39
    counselor's use of, 38-41, 81-82, 84,
        87, 95-99, 117-125
    goal of therapy, 4-10, 27, 32-34, 53,
        68, 71
    historical, 12-13, 143-146
    humanistic psychology and, 8-10, 35,
        98-99
    of cultural feminists, 16-17
    of liberal feminists, 14
    of radical feminists, 15, 30
    of socialist feminists, 15-16, 50, 147
    personal healing from, 9, 117, 119,
        126, 129-131, 139
    See also Counseling study; Subversive
        counseling
African Americans. *See* Black nationalists;
    Black women
Agoraphobia, 36

Alcohol abuse, 81
Alienation, 7-8
Alternative feminist systems, 28-29, 147
    See also Battered women's shelters
American Psychological Association
    (APA), 31
Anger:
    management techniques, 64
    use of, 32-33, 40, 51-53
Antipsychiatrists, 6-7, 71
Anti-rape movement, 28, 48, 50
    See also Sexual violence
Assault. *See* Domestic violence; Sexual
    violence
Assertiveness training, 36, 61, 65
Association for Women in Psychology
    (AWP), 31
Atkinson, Ti-Grace, 146

Backlash, against women, 123, 132, 141
Battered women:
    as accomplices to abuse, 63
    as survivors, 27, 51, 67-68, 80, 114-115
    case studies of, 1-3, 129-131
    economic dependence of, 52, 61, 111

About the Author

Mollie Whalen is Coordinator of Women's Studies and Director of the Women's Center at East Stroudsburg University, Pennsylvania. She is an Assistant Professor in the Department of Counseling and Educational Opportunity. She obtained her undergraduate degree in psychology from East Stroudsburg University (1978). She holds a master's in clinical psychology from Fairleigh Dickinson University (1980) and a Ph.D. from New York University's counseling psychology program (1992).

Her scholarly efforts, as a feminist psychologist and a women's studies coordinator, are directed toward building connections between feminist theory and praxis. She recently coauthored a paper with Patricia Graham, "(WO)MENtoring and As(SISTER)ing: Building Power Among African American Women in the Academy," to be published in Black Women in the Academy: Defending Our Name 1894-1994. She participated in the NGO Forum of the United Nations Fourth World Conference on Women, in Beijing, as part of the Association for Women in Psychology.

For nearly 15 years, she worked in the battered women's and anti-rape social movements. From 1984 to 1990, she was the director of Women's Resources of Monroe County, a community-based rape and domestic violence program, and a board member of the Pennsylvania Coalition Against Domestic Violence and the Pennsylvania Coalition Against Rape.